READING WITHIN AND
BEYOND THE CLASSROOM

Open University Press

English, Language, and Education series

General Editor: Anthony Adams

Lecturer in Education, University of Cambridge

This series is concerned with all aspects of language in education
from the primary school to the tertiary sector. Its authors are
experienced educators who examine both principles and practice of
English subject teaching and language across the curriculum in the
context of current educational and societal developments.

TITLES IN THE SERIES

READING WITHIN AND BEYOND THE CLASSROOM

Dan Taverner

Open University Press
Milton Keynes · Philadelphia

To Dorothy

Open University Press
Celtic Court
22 Ballmoor
Buckingham MK18 1XW
and
1900 Frost Road, Suite 101
Bristol, PA 19007, USA

First Published 1990

British Library Cataloguing in Publication Data

Taverner, Dan
    Reading within and beyond the classroom. – (English,
    language, and education series)
    1. Schools curriculum subjects: reading: Teaching
    I. Title   II. Series
    428'.4'071

    ISBN 0-335-09579-8

Library of Congress Cataloging-in-Publication Data

Taverner, D. T. (Dan T.)
    Reading within and beyond the classroom/Dan Taverner.
        p.   cm.
    Includes bibliographical references.
    ISBN 0-335-09579-8
    1. Reading (Elementary)—Great Britain.   I. Title.
LB1573.T349   1990
372.4'0941—dc20   89-48396
                                            CIP

Typeset by Rowland Phototypesetting Limited
Bury St Edmunds, Suffolk
Printed in Great Britain by St Edmundsbury Press Limited
Bury St Edmunds, Suffolk

Contents

General editor's introduction

Dan Taverner is already likely to be known by many of the most immediate potential readers of this book. He was for many years an Inspector of Schools with the London Borough of Newham, from where he recently retired with the rank of Senior Inspector. He was founder-Chair of the National Association for Advisers in Education (NAAE) and remains their President. Since his retirement he has been assisting with the work of the English Methods course in the Cambridge University PGCE course and remains closely in touch with all aspects of the teaching of English, at a national as well as local level. He has also been awarded an OBE for his services to education.

Essentially a modest and hard-working man, Dan will not be especially pleased to have this biographical note as the opening of this introduction. It seems to me important to realize, however, the extent to which this book could only have come out of the author's close personal involvement with the mainstream of English teaching. In his national role he has been involved in the preparation of evidence to every enquiry into the teaching of English from the Bullock Report (*A Language for Life*, HMSO, 1975) to that of the Cox Working Group on English in the National Curriculum (*English 5–16*, HMSO, 1989). Responses to this latter report are being prepared even as I write this introduction. It will be clear from the text of the book that Dan, like many of us, would feel that there is still much in Bullock of the greatest relevance to our present concerns in language teaching, not least in the field of reading teaching. But there is much in Cox also that echoes Bullock, and Dan, along with myself, greatly welcomes the good sense that underlies much of the Cox recommendations. If there appears to be something of a mismatch between the excellent review of good current practice in classrooms and the sometimes vaguely and awkwardly phrased Attainment Targets, this is not entirely the fault of the Working Group. Indeed, their explicit recognition of the difficulty of putting age-related targets to English teaching (14.5) indicates the impossibility of their task.

The fact of our working in the same office has meant that I have had a closer than usual awareness of the evolution of the present volume whilst it has been in the process of writing. However, when the final manuscript arrived on my desk, even I was astonished at the up-to-dateness that it represented. The book grows out of a lifetime's professional involvement with the teaching of reading: yet every section is introduced and supported by a relevant quotation from the Report of the Cox Working Group. In itself this should be helpful to teachers of language, struggling to turn the new National Curriculum into classroom applications. Under the terms of Cox at least, it remains possible to continue good classroom practice. Indeed, if the recommendations of the Report were universally implemented in the schools, there would be an immediate rise in overall standards. This book, shows in the important area of reading, how this may be achieved. In these pages teachers will find chapter and verse from the latest recommendations to the government to support the best of classroom and home practices in reading development.

The book grows naturally out of Dan Taverner's earlier work, *Developing a Reading Programme* (Ward Lock Educational, 1980). That book was a close look at reading in the primary school and drew, in a typically eclectic way, upon the best of research and practice which teachers could implement in their own classrooms. I know it has been found helpful by many teachers with whom I have worked personally on in-service courses. Indeed, because of its awareness of the classroom realities that lie behind reading theory, I found myself recommending the book to my PGCE trainees preparing to teach in secondary schools, where, so often, the actual teaching of reading and higher reading skills has been sorely neglected. It was its usefulness in this respect that made me feel that the book needed bringing up to date and expanding. I also especially wanted Dan to include something about the continuity of reading teaching between primary and secondary schooling. All this led me to press Dan into writing the present book. In doing so, he has produced, however, a totally new book. In particular the emphasis on continuity in the reading programme that I was seeking for, took on the extra dimension of the need for continuity between home and school reading, concerns that sprang directly out of his work in the London Borough of Newham. It was work in that area also, that led to the increasing emphasis on the multi-cultural dimension of teaching reading that will be found in this book.

Reading has been, arguably, the most academically researched area of the language curriculum. Whole courses in North American universities and in this country have been devoted to how it should be taught. Notably, in the UK, we have had the very influential Open University Diploma in Reading Development, which ran for many years with a transforming effect on the teaching of reading in British primary schools. It has also never been far from public debate and professional acrimony with strong advocates of different methods as the only true road to reading. These debates have been important – even if they have had the unfortunate effect of polarization at times – for they have all, in their way, informed the best of practice of good teachers, who have started not with theories but with the children in their classroom. Infant teachers, in particular, are wise in taking from theory whatever is good for their children based upon their extensive practical experience. What most authorities are agreed upon from Wilkinson in *The Foundations of Language* (Oxford University Press, 1971) to Bullock, and now to Dan Taverner, is that the approach to reading teaching has to be essentially eclectic: to put it simply the best 'method' of teaching reading is the one that works and this usually means also the one that the teacher believes in for that child.

But there are two other things that seem important. One of these is the necessity to provide a climate for reading in the classroom, a 'book-filled environment' at the very least. The importance of this and its practical implications are dealt with here as well as in, what may be considered a companion book in the series, Barrie Wade's *Reading for Real* (Open University Press, 1989) which shares much common ground with Taverner.

The other element that seems essential to me has already been mentioned, that is continuity. Arguably, one of the important effects of the National Curriculum will be to ensure much more continuity in language programmes as pupils proceed through the various levels. Most books on the teaching of reading tend to be read by primary specialists only. It was because of this that I wanted Dan to bridge the phase divides between infant/junior and junior/secondary education in the present book. To this he has added the equally important bridging of the divide between the home and the school reading programmes and the child's developing experiences, expectations and processes of reading. In doing this, Dan has written a book that should be found useful by teachers at all levels of the educational system as well as by parents. It would be entirely in accordance with the spirit of the book that it should be widely read by the general as well as the specialized public. Teachers might even find it a useful starting point for a series of meetings with parents on reading within the National Curriculum.

With this in mind the book has been written with admirable clarity and good sense. Years of committee work have enabled Dan to process dense material into clear common sense language. The whole work is informed by a wealth of scholarship but it is a scholarship that sits easily on the author's shoulders. Those who need to know where reading stands today will find much to inform and to delight in the following pages.

Anthony Adams

Acknowledgements

I wish to record my thanks to colleagues in the London Borough of Newham whose experiences are reflected in this book. In particular I wish to acknowledge the contributions of Mr Angelides and Mrs Brien of the Language Reading Team, the Headteachers' Steering Group and the many teachers who are working in the Newham Reading Project. I wish also to thank the Authority for the support it has afforded me. My thanks and appreciation go to Tony Adams for his sound advice as general editor of this series.

Introduction

In the last few years there have been more fundamental changes in education than ever previously experienced by serving teachers. These changes follow a growing concern that arises mainly from outside the teaching profession but which is increasingly beginning to influence the profession itself. This concern over educational standards, which started with economic considerations, value for money and accountability, reached its climax in the 1988 Education Reform Act. The effects of this measure are increasingly being felt in schools not least by its influence upon the curriculum which the Secretary of State called the 'bedrock' of his policy. Programmes of Study (PoS), with their associated Attainment Targets (ATs), are being introduced into schools in September 1989 for key stage 1 (5–7 years), and other programmes will begin to be phased in for subsequent stages.

Within the recommendations of the various curriculum working groups, reading still maintains its central position. It could well be, however, that increasing pressures on schools will have a narrowing down effect upon what is taught. It was the possibility of such a curriculum 'straitjacket' that Sir Keith Joseph complained of when the Act was being debated.

It is important, then, to reaffirm the broad view that many teachers have of the reading process, and to be successful this reaffirmation must be supported with a clear rationale. This book attempts to provide such a rationale and will begin with a consideration of existing broad – and often disparate – views of reading. From these different perspectives it will attempt to draw out a cohesive reading programme.

1 Some perspectives on reading

Reading is more than the decoding of black marks upon a page: it is a quest for meaning and one which requires the reader to be an active participant (DES, 1988b, 16.2).

Reading was the first 'R' and, under the Revised Code, a teacher forfeited 2s 8d for every scholar's failure to satisfy the Inspector in reading, which at the time was concerned largely with the matching of sounds with symbols.

Although 'payment by results' officially died at the beginning of this century, it has refused to be buried and its shadow is still with us, possibly resurfacing to a greater extent in recent years. It was in operation during the formative years of our educational system and branded teachers' attitudes: it conditioned thinking towards the quantitative evaluation of children's work with the implication that what could be measured was important and, conversely, what could not be tested was peripheral.

This thinking has tended to perpetuate the concept of reading as being largely concerned with the reproduction of 'correct' sounds, with the associated importance of normative reading tests and reading ages. As early as 1906, however, Welton stated that:

> The method of teaching reading which harmonises with the method of learning is one which begins with words, which connects writing with reading, which introduces phonic analysis later as a help to the recognition of other words and, above all, which treats reading indeed as the understanding of visible talking.

Such attitudes, expressed in teachers' handbooks over 80 years ago – many of which would be a part of today's thinking – reveal the extent to which successive generations have been conditioned to the teach–test approach. This thinking includes the 'parcels of learning' belief, which made necessary the well-known 'activity and experience' statement of the Hadow Report in the 1930s.

Despite the large amount of classroom time being spent on reading, there was concern over standards as early as the First World War. Army authorities noted the inability of conscripts to read, something that was magnified when the men were demobbed. Similar concerns were expressed during the Second World War and at the time of National Service.

With the launch of the USSR's first orbital satellite, Sputnik 1, on 4 October 1957, it was recognized that greater attention needed to be paid to literacy. In order to develop a competitive technology, it was necessary to foster a scientific bias in education and, consequently, an ability to read technical journals.

There is a tendency for concerns over reading to assume patterns – often cyclical in nature – which reflect society's interest in education and which is now crystallized in the 1988 Act.

The education system is undergoing many changes and parents are receiving much bewildering and sometimes contradictory information. Many parents reason that reading, at least, remains unaltered, for everyone knows about reading! They tend to cling to this thought, for reading is one of the few areas of the curriculum that they feel they have had direct experience of. 'Modern' maths, IT and creative work tend to present parents with difficulties of interpretation and, consequently, of assessment.

Reading then, tends to be one of the main criteria by which the education system is judged. It is also true to say that never has there been a greater interest in education and, therefore, in reading. Judgements often tend to be related to the extent to which children appear to progress along reading schemes or, in some cases, to whether they 'know their letters'. This restrictive view often produces restricted comments and, at least as far as some members of the media are concerned, 'bad news is good news'.

On a wider scale, the question of accountability is increasingly being raised. The feeling that what is achieved in education must be justified in terms of the financial demands placed on rate- and taxpayers, again tends to emphasize those curricular aspects which appear to be most readily measurable. At this level, also, has been the debate over 'permissiveness', and successful reading has been linked with forceful teaching and discipline; conversely, an inability to read is often associated with too much freedom, too many frills and too much creative work.

In the past, reading, as well as being the responsibility of teachers, has involved educational psychologists whose interests lay in remediation. More recently, linguists and sociologists have made important contributions and have thus broadened the field of interest. As a result, the number of research projects and publications concerned with the learning and teaching of reading has increased, particularly in the wake of the 1988 Reform Act. This has meant that people have had to be more selective in their reading. There is a natural tendency to read summaries which, by their very nature, are not always able to present a balanced view. Reports of this kind tend to emphasize those aspects that appear more dramatic and, therefore, they often give further impetus to the current concerns of many over reading abilities.

In 1987, an article in *The Times* began with the statement: 'A mother of three children has devised a scheme which teaches children to read independently in a week but her ideas have been rejected by up to forty publishers.' In October of that year, *The Times* reported on a reading test which would be a 'New reading age guide to parents.' The author of the test stated that it 'should not be interpreted in terms of a measure of intelligence, creativity, examination potential, or anything else beyond the ability to make sense of the written word'.

These comments reflect some restricted views of reading, which is still seen by many as the ability to put sounds with letters and to make the appropriate noises. In *Our Mutual Friend* (1864), Boffin, when being taught to read, talks about the process as 'A shovelin' an' siftin' of alphabeds.' Referring to this sound–symbol matching, the Bullock Report (DES, 1975) states that the belief that reading 'Consists of matching sounds and symbols in some simple way is therefore quite untenable. Teaching techniques based solely on this assumption can hamper subsequent reading development.'

There is no suggestion here that these phonic techniques should be ignored, but any view of reading needs to go beyond this and to accept that it is a much broader and more subtle activity. As *The Times* article commented, it involves 'The ability to make sense of the written word' – but this is only part of it. At the age of 74, Goethe said that he was still learning to read, 'although I have been at it all my life'. He saw reading as a personal 'responsive' process that is essentially a pleasurable experience. This view of reading is echoed by Bernard Levin: 'The pleasures of reading are innocent, inexhaustible, incomparable, incalculable, and infinite, and no one who can read at all is shut out from enjoying them' (*The Sunday Times*, 6 November 1983). If reading is all this, it is no easy task to describe it, and nor can this be a particularly fruitful activity for, as Marion Jenkinson (1972) says, 'After 75 years of research and investigation, there has not emerged a cohesive construct within which we can examine reading.'

Nevertheless, teachers are constantly faced with the task of sharing their views on reading with colleagues and others outside the profession. The extension of links with schools and their communities, the changing role of school management and increased parental involvement, together with many other aspects of the 1988 Act, are all resulting in teachers being much more in the limelight. This need to share their insights into children's reading development will be particularly important when the results of assessment measures are made known. Therefore, the need for teachers to have their own rationale that underpins their teaching of reading has never been more obvious. This must include attention to reading as being a part of the whole language process.

Reading and experience

Reading takes pupils beyond first-hand experience: it enables them to project themselves into unfamiliar environments, times and cultures, to gain sympathetic understanding of other ways of life and to experience joy and sadness vicariously (DES, 1988b, 16.3).

Through the act of reading, meaning can be set against experience. It is a way of coming to terms with the past and offers opportunities of accommodating to and

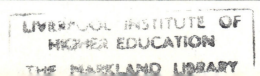

then of assimilating past experiences. It is a fact that many people who have undergone traumatic experiences feel the need, once they are secure, to read about them. This often enables them to put what has happened into some form of perspective. Many children, for example, who have had to attend hospital or who have experienced crises at home, find a need to read about them. In this context, reading can be a very private activity.

The desire to review the past is a very natural one and reading about past experiences offers opportunities for recalling and savouring them. James Britton (1970) once likened words to 'filing pins' that can be used to reorder thinking about what has happened, and in doing so the reader is able to confirm and validate those experiences. The Bullock Report (DES, 1975) comments that a reader 'draws reassurance from realising that his personal difficulties and his feelings of deficiency are not unique to himself'. This kind of reassurance, in which reading is used as a personal resource, is particularly important for children.

Reading can also be used as a means of extending experience: 'It presents a child with controlled experience which he can observe from the outside at the same time as being involved within it' (DES, 1975). This is perhaps why children still love to read about 'monsters', and why they enjoy some fairy tales and science fiction stories, which become the raw materials for their fantasies to work on: they can retreat from the story if it gets too frightening and re-engage with it when they feel safe.

Reading and learning

This use of reading as a means of extending experience is, of course, an important part of the learning process. Reading requires you to think, which calls for the ability to anticipate outcomes, and then to confirm, to modify or to reject them:

> Reading constantly subjects the reader's mind to new information requiring him to adjust his thinking. Thus the reader's progress through a story is marked by a steady change of ideas. Each word, each fact, each concept, each line or sentence requires a reader to react, accept, reject, associate and assimilate (Stauffer and Cramer, 1968).

Some reading 'models'

Much of what has been said so far fits into Edgar Dale's broad pattern of reading (Strang, 1978), in which he considered the now familiar concept of three interconnected and overlapping stages of reading. The first, 'reading the lines', is concerned with extracting the literal meaning from the text. It involves the ability to decode and to focus on key words and word sequences. The second of Dale's levels, 'reading between the lines', involves a degree of critical reading. This means assessing the purposes of the authors, following their lines of argument and making judgements about their views and conclusions. It can then lead to comparative reading in which these conclusions are matched with those of others and the drawing of distinctions between facts and opinions. 'Reading beyond the lines' is the most developed stage in this model. It involves extending the scope of some of the authors' ideas, of reshaping them and setting them against the experiences of the reader. It is a personal and responsive stage that involves reflections and evaluations.

These views of reading are summed up by Ruth Strang (1978), when she says that:

> Reading is more than seeing words clearly, more than pronouncing words correctly, more than recognizing the meaning of isolated words. Reading requires you to think, feel and imagine. Effective reading is purposeful.

Reading then is seen as a complex and many-dimensional personal activity. In order to come to terms with these concepts of the process, it is necessary to examine how they can be applied to a reading structure.

2 A reading structure

Reading, then, cannot be learned or taught in a week, and for its successful development it involves the attitudes, skills and expectations of the teachers and of the children themselves (these influencing factors will be considered in more detail on pp. 22–41. Reading is a complex process, but it *is* a process and it is developmental. It is possible in mathematics and science to chart certain clear and progressive steps in a linear way, but because of this complexity it cannot be done satisfactorily with reading. How then is it possible to arrive at a structure for the learning and teaching of reading that teachers can build and use? In any programme there are certain significant 'focal points' that can be identified. These are not only seen as 'milestones' that indicate certain important stages reached, but also as signposts pointing to future stages and directions. In the reading process these range from the pre-book stage to that of Dale's 'reading beyond the lines'.

If these stages are identified, they can present a framework for reading acquisition that will provide a structure upon which a reading programme can be built. What are these important focal points?

Pre-reading

Reading activities should build on the oral language and experiences which pupils bring from home (DES, 1988b, 16.22).

Young fluent readers

In *Young Fluent Readers*, Margaret Clark (1976) studied 32 children who were able to read when starting school at the age of 5, and she identified a number of factors which contributed to their success. Increasingly, it is being accepted by the 'professionals' that parents are the first teachers and that they are often very successful ones, and that early schooling needs to take an informed account of what happens to children before they arrive in school. This is generally easier to undertake in a nursery school or unit where the main provision for part-time children encourages liaison with parents and where pre-school home visiting is adopted. A great many infant and first schools, however, have also done a great deal to encourage family liaison (see pp. 60–70). The 'fluent' children in Clark's seminal book received their support from home, but the sound practices which she considers are those which many good schools are also using.

She mentions the importance of encouraging spoken language through finding time as an 'interested adult' to listen to children and to respond to them: 'Few of the parents had consciously attempted to teach their children to read' she says, but what they had done was to share with them their love of books and to provide 'lap time' when they read to them and shared a book with them.

Young children and books

These parents were convinced that reading in its broadest, pleasurable sense was important to them, and that this attitude to books was caught by their children. As one teacher once remarked on a course, 'We need to be seen as "reading teachers" as well as teachers of reading.' Through this sharing of books, children begin to recognize that pictures can be 'read' and that illustrations can tell stories. They learn how to handle a book and its physical characteristics. Bernard Levin said that his first friends were books and discusses 'The sensual pleasure' in book handling. 'I am', he says in *The Sunday Times*, 'An incurable book sniffer.' This attitude is noticeable in younger children, particularly if they feel that the book is their own property.

Through the use of school bookshops, parents' centres and the increase in the number of book outlets, including supermarkets, there are more opportunities than ever for children to own their own small 'libraries'. Book ownership enables children to go back time and again to a favourite book, to learn to turn its pages and talk about it, to begin to develop an idea of sequence, and to begin to anticipate story developments.

Book sharing with adults encourages children to start asking questions about the print. They begin to learn that those black squiggles are significant and start to identify some individual letters. They also begin to realize that separate words exist and that when we talk it is made up of these units. This leads them to discuss words themselves and begin on the path towards 'Knowledge about Language', one of the concerns of the Kingman Inquiry (DES, 1988a).

Early language

The pre-reading stage is not too early to start these sorts of discussions. Katherine Perera (1987) suggests that there is a tendency for us to underestimate the amount of language which a 5-year-old has learned: by that age, 'Most English speaking children have a vocabulary of at least 2,000 words and have mastered many hundreds of grammatical constructions.'

One of the most important ways of early language learning arises from the range of activities that children undertake at home and in nursery schools. These play sessions can be used to give purpose and context to stories, rhymes and pictures. They are also important in their own right as developing qualities that are important to the reading process. These include commitment to the activity for its own sake, repetition and cooperation, which is a necessary part of the author–reader relationship.

Beginning reading

> *It is a perquisite of successful teaching of reading, especially in the early stages, that whenever techniques are taught, or books chosen for children's use, meaning should always be in the foreground* (DES, 1988b, 16.2).

These early experiences support the sense of pleasure, security and purpose that can be derived from books and can provide a firm foundation for future development.

Reading readiness

One of the outcomes of the growth in child-centred education was the development of the concept of 'readiness'. It was argued that, until a child was ready for a certain stage, there was no point in attempting to teach it. In its broadest interpretation, this does of course make sense: a child cannot be expected to swim a length unless he or she has the confidence to float; and a 6-year-old cannot be expected to read the *Encyclopaedia Britannica* with any great enthusiasm.

There was a feeling, however, that this 'readiness' grew naturally and at its own pace. Many teachers were sceptical of this view, for they believed that however 'rich' the class environment, children would not necessarily learn a great deal from it simply by being immersed in it. It is possible for children to be surrounded by books but, if left to their own devices, they would not necessarily read them.

Many teachers welcomed the Bullock Report's comments on their role of 'planned intervention' and supported its comments on readiness:

> It cannot be emphasised too strongly that the teacher has to help children towards readiness for beginning reading. There is no question of waiting for readiness to occur; for with many children it does not come 'naturally' and must be brought about by the teachers' positive measures to induce it (DES, 1975).

Teacher intervention

In accepting this statement we need to ask about the ways in which teachers can intervene at this stage and what are the 'positive measures' to which Bullock refers. Frank Smith (1971) states quite categorically that 'Basically a child is equipped with every skill that he needs in order to read; all that he needs to discover are the particular rules that apply.' This links with Perera's view (p. 7) of the extent of the knowledge of words and constructions that many 5-year-olds have. It is possible to consider a long list of these 'rules' and many of them will be discussed in greater detail when reading methods are examined (see Chapter 4).

In more general terms, however, they can be included under the broad headings of language about language, language patterns and story conventions, syntax, and the ability to manipulate symbols. Smith (1971) suggests that these rules will need to be 'induced' by the child from the raw material that the teacher presents as examples: 'What the child has to do is to predict a regularity on the basis of information received on one occasion and try it out to see if the role is valid on another occasion.' He sees the teacher's role as one of providing information and feedback.

Stories and rhymes

One of the most valuable ways of providing children with these sorts of experiences at all stages is by using stories and rhymes of all kinds. Through listening to these, children begin to acquire patterns of language. They begin to get the feel of words and begin to appreciate that certain words come in sequence (we don't say 'Three mice blind') and that the order of words can alter the meanings they carry. They begin to accept that sets of words hang together and to recognize any disruption in the pattern when words are deliberately used out of sequence. This presents opportunities for playing with words and encouraging the 'inducement' of the rules as Smith suggests. These patterns, which many children build through listening to narrative, also include a growing awareness of the conventions of stories and rhymes. Children begin to recognize and come to expect a certain order of things and to expect stories to develop in certain ways, once the nature of the main characters has been established. They begin to anticipate and then to predict the story line and get some satisfaction if these predictions are realized, or surprise if this does not happen and if there is a twist in the story. This ability to predict is, of course, a quality which is needed at every stage of reading.

Through the repetition of nursery rhymes and stories, children begin to know the word orders in the text by heart, and if the book has been read to a group by the teacher it acquires an added status and many children want to see it and handle it themselves. In doing this they often repeat what they have heard and go through the motions of reading it. This is an important part of the beginning reading stage. A few years ago, concern was expressed over the belief that many children were not experiencing fairy tales and nursery rhymes. Today, this concern has less foundation and to the traditional tales is being added a richness of stories from many other cultures. This concern reflected the important part these play in children's development. In talking about fairy tales, Opie and Opie (1976) say that:

The magic sets us wondering how we our selves would act in similar circumstances. It encourages speculation, it gives a child licence to wonder and this is the merit of these tales that by going beyond possibility they enlarge our daily horizon.

This 'licence to wonder' is important to all stages of reading, particularly when children become independent voluntary readers.

Storytelling

Another dimension to children and narrative is added when adults tell them stories. On these occasions, there is no possibility of the book coming between the adult and the child and a stronger personal relationship is often the result. Storytelling is an art and a valuable teaching skill, often involving the uses of dramatic skills, including timing and significant pauses. Using the voice to add rhythm and variations in pitch sets the mood of the story. Is it serious, is it funny, or is it scary? This enables the children to put the story into a known context and they are often ready to join in when recognizing word sequences and well-known story lines. These are also the sort of 'rules' which Frank Smith (1971) may have had in mind.

The flexibility of storytelling and the important part it plays in early reading is summed up by Ralph Lavender when he refers to the desire of children themselves to undertake what he calls 'storying'. He suggests that through listening to stories and through the enjoyment they engender, 'Each child will discover the real urge to become literate' (NATE, 1979).

It is at this beginning stage when many long-term attitudes to reading are formed and it is important that they should be associated with a view of reading as an exciting and enjoyable activity. The positive attitudes of children that arise from the feelings of pleasure and of purpose which books can provide are an essential part of the next 'focal point' in the reading framework.

Supported reading

Teachers should recognise that reading is a complex but unitary process and not a set of discrete skills which can be taught separately in turn and, ultimately, bolted together (DES, 1988b, 16.9).

Learning to read as a process has been compared with learning to drive, in that there are certain skills which need to be acquired. In both cases, these depend upon attitudes for their application and, to be successful, need to be applied with a sense of purpose and of understanding. In order to learn to drive, the guidance and advice of an instructor is necessary. With reading, encouragement, support and direction are needed from the teacher. This support includes making appropriate books and materials available. In many schools, the beginning stages of reading lead into the uses of reading schemes, with their associated activities, and to a sharper focus on more specific aspects of the reading of individual children.

Reading schemes

Many schools use reading schemes as a core around which are clustered many of the books held within the school. The ways in which they may be organized and some of the methods in which they are used will be considered on pp. 31–3.

Starting on a reading scheme is seen by many children and their parents as being an important stage, marking the child's first step in reading. There is often some confusion about what a 'scheme' is, but it is generally accepted as being a series of basic books which are numbered according to predetermined levels of difficulty. This means that a child's movement through a reading scheme tends to be used to indicate his or her general progress in reading.

Schools are encouraging a broader view than this through extending the scope of their core books and linking them with an increasingly wide range of other books and materials. As one headteacher comments in the Thomas Report (ILEA, 1985): 'It is hoped that these support materials will encourage children and parents to see reading in its broadest sense and not just in association with the next book level.' A basic scheme, however, is still considered by many schools to be central to the reading process at this stage. It is argued that the use of a clearly defined scheme also provides a support structure for teachers and, in particular, for those in their early years in the profession.

Whatever schemes are used, it is important for teachers to be aware of the principles upon which any grading is based. They also need to know about the approaches adopted: Are they phonically based? Do they use language experience approaches? Are they a combination of a number of these? What are some of the questions which need to be resolved? In assessing the purposes of a particular scheme in this way, and in examining its strengths and weaknesses, it is often necessary to study any accompanying handbook. There is also a clear need for the teacher to keep 'alongside the child' as progress is made. This book-sharing with children of all ages is among the most important activities that a teacher can undertake and means careful planning if it is to be successful.

Whatever organization a teacher adopts, it is increasingly clear that there is a need for children to understand the purposes behind the task. In its evidence to the House of Commons Select Committee on Achievement in Primary Education, the British Psychological Society (1986) stated:

> Success with a problem now seems to depend more on the way the task is presented and on children's understanding of what they have to do than was formerly realised. Pupils' progress is therefore seen to be sensitive to teachers' choices of content and task.

While working through a book with a child, the question 'Why are we doing this?' is a valid one to raise from time to time.

It is important, then, for children to be aware of what they are about and the idea that the reading purpose is 'to get to the end of the book so that I can start on the next number' needs to be challenged. It reflects a view by the child that these are not real books but rather a series of pre-set exercises. Many recent publications, however, have an increased flexibility and many teachers see the uses of reading schemes as only part of a range of activities.

Letters and sounds

Among the 'rules' which Frank Smith (1971) discussed, he included the need for the child 'to learn what are the distinctive features of written language and their relations to letters and words and meanings'. As children move into this stage of supported reading, many of them will focus upon words and their make-up and a number will ask for, and will need, support in coping with them. As was said at the beginning of this book, reading is far more than the linking of sounds with letters and there is not always any direct match between the way in which the English language is written and the way it sounds. At the same time, a great many teachers see the need for some form of attention to phonics at a particular stage. Many feel that this attention is closely linked with the demands of reading schemes. A number feel that to encourage success with a particular book a child should be prepared for it through working with particular words and phrases before attempting to read it.

Whenever it is undertaken, it is generally accepted that handling phonics is not necessarily an easy option (see Chapter 4). It involves a number of stages which include isolating the word, breaking it down into its component symbols, matching these with their appropriate sounds, and then putting them together again. This process of analysis and synthesis needs careful support from the teacher and the timing of its introduction is an important consideration. As the Bullock Report (DES, 1975) comments: 'The question then is not whether or not to teach phonics, of this there can be no doubt. The question is how and when to do it.' In tackling phonics it is important for teachers to be aware of the dangers of teaching them as isolated skills. In its evidence to the Kingman Committee, the Cambridge Seminar (1987) stated that:

> A fragmented approach to language learning built upon a concept of language as a collection of sub-skills which can be taught in isolation and tested through discrete exercises will lead to an impairment of children's language growth.

The learning of phonics, then, needs to take place in the context of purpose and meaning with the acquired skill being applied to the solution of a specific and real problem. There are dangers in teaching phonics in separation and as a programme in their own right, for there is little evidence to show that children transfer this learning to their own broader reading (this will be examined in greater detail in Chapter 4).

Reading on

There have been tendencies to taper off more direct support in reading once children have progressed through a basic 'scheme'. HMI say in their Report on Primary Education (DES, 1978) that:

It is evident that teachers devoted considerable attention to ensuring that children mastered the basic techniques in reading but there was a tendency at all ages for children to receive insufficient encouragement to extend the range of their reading.

In the 9–13 Middle School Survey (DES, 1983a), HMI commented that in only a small number of schools was children's reading being 'systematically extended'. Two years later, the 8–12 HMI Survey (DES, 1985a) found that only in about half the schools reviewed was attention being given to this extension. The majority of teachers do now appear to accept that planned reading support should not come to an end when a child leaves an infant or a first school and they are using a number of tactics to maintain this support.

One challenge which is beginning to be met lies at the 'infant–junior interface', when children move from one stage to the next with the possibilities of facing changes in expectations of achievement as well as of methods and organizations. Where separate schools exist, liaison policies need to be worked out carefully and agreed upon. A number of schools feel that there is still some way to go in this direction. A number of children when transferring from infant to junior schools still need the attention referred to. These children could well be 'two-year infants', who because their birthdays fell after Easter, could not be accepted as rising 5's and therefore would not start school until the following September. This is only one of a number of factors (e.g. illness and absences, changes of school, etc.) that could inhibit development and which underline the importance of continued support into the junior or middle schools.

The tendency, however, for many of the children who have not completed a 'basic scheme' to be labelled as remedial at this stage is now much less noticeable. Successful early junior teaching is being increasingly based upon good infant practice and developed from that.

In order to consider this aspect of continued reading, a four-year, school-based project was established by the then Schools Council. Southgate *et al.* (1981), working with practising teachers, considered the reading of children in the 7–9+ age range. They produced some interesting findings which are worth examining. They found, for example, that some children of average reading ability in this age range 'had, by the end of the year, made considerably less progress than might have been anticipated'. They go on to say that the most successful classes devoted a greater proportion of their time to children's uninterrupted personal reading and less time to listening to individual children read. In examining this aspect, the authors found that as a result of constant interruptions, the average time that teachers were able to give their full attention to individual children's reading was no more than 30 seconds on each occasion. It recommends that there should be a greater span of time allocated to working with individual children (15–20 minutes). This implies a review of the weekly time allowed for reading and a close look at the organizational problems involved. Many of the practical and organizational aspects of these suggestions will be examined in greater detail in Chapter 4.

The reading climate

Attitudes

Running through much of what has been discussed so far is the importance attached to supporting positive attitudes towards reading growth and habits of reading. The APU, in its second Primary Survey Report on Language Perform- ance in Schools (DES, 1981a), examines the attitudes to reading of 11-year-olds in the belief that 'These attitudes will already be affecting the use they make of their reading skills and the reading activities they voluntarily engage in.' The language monitoring team found that of the 1000 pupils questioned, the great majority saw reading in functional terms. Many saw the need to read as a means of coping with the demands of school and others accepted reading as a means of determining future employment. A number of other 11-year-olds in this sample felt that learning to read was a means of preparing for everyday life and quoted such examples as reading letters, reading labels on tins when shopping, reading posters, timetables and 'important documents'. A smaller number saw reading as a means of increasing knowledge and only 13% referred to reading as a source of entertainment and enjoyment.

These attitudes often reflect the views of children's families, of their peer groups and of some of the media. In order to encourage broader attitudes to reading, particularly at this 'supportive stage', it is necessary to take account of these views and, in particular, those of parents.

The great majority of parents are very interested in their children's reading. They may not always reveal this because many are conditioned by their own school experiences, when teaching was often seen as a closed professional task. Now schools and their classrooms are generally much more open and welcoming, but a number of parents (though this is rapidly decreasing) are still uncertain of how to get 'into the system'. An important task facing all teachers (discussed in more detail on pp. 66–70 is that of sharing their views on reading with parents. This could well include the belief that 'pragmatic reading' is just one part of a broader process which also includes reading for enjoyment.

Atmosphere

To the support of worthwhile reading habits and attitudes, the 'reading atmos- phere' of a school and its individual classrooms make essential contributions. This begins when reading is put at the centre of many activities and in accepting that, at whatever level of working, 'every teacher is a teacher of reading'. Christopher Walker (1974) states that:

> It is essential to give reading in post-infant schools the sort of status which it obviously has at the infant stage. Here the most basic of all school subjects, it is regarded as a subject in its own right. It needs to be so regarded in Junior, Middle and Secondary schools.

Accepting the central importance of reading at all levels implies making available a range of attractive books that are thoughtfully displayed and encour- age their uses by children. The linking of books to a range of school activities, the setting up of displays and exhibitions and the mounting of wall charts and pictures are all ways of encouraging a reading atmosphere. Most important is to devise opportunities for talking to children about books. In the development of a school climate, these 'book discussions' can include the contributions of visitors from other classes within the school or from the community that supports the school.

An example of this, which is similar to the supported reading approach adopted by a number of schools, was a talk given to a fourth-year junior class by a local pensioner. He was able to talk about his own schooling and to use a book display which had been set up by a borough librarian. The display was one of books used in the 1920s and 1930s and the visitor was able to show some of the newspapers he had kept from the war. He shared with the children some of the comics he had read as a boy and a few of the treasured books that were an important part of his life. This visit started a series of follow-up activities concerned with books and the important part they play in the lives of many people.

Independent reading

The requirement to make time for independent reading, not least as a source of pleasure, remains crucial, whatever the total curriculum demands (DES, 1988b, 16.5).

The nature of support in reading and its intensity and direction will change as children develop and their needs become more complex. Mackay *et al.* (1970) comment in the teachers' manual *Breakthrough to Literacy* that a child 'must learn to become skilled in a private, solitary activity where he has been used to a public social activity'. The adoption of this 'private' aspect of reading, which is usually voluntary, can be regarded as an important 'milestone' occupying a key position in the reading framework.

In its second Primary Survey Report (of 1982) (DES, 1984(a)), the APU states that 'The crux of learning to read is the independent use made by pupils of their reading skills', and the importance of this personal commitment to reading is emphasized in the Thomas Report. In his report, Norman Thomas says that children will not become readers by choice 'unless from the beginning of the process they are accustomed to think of reading as something to be done for a personal reason and not simply to please an adult' (ILEA, 1985).

From these and many other sources there is a great deal of support for the need to foster the development of pupils' independent reading. The second APU report (DES, 1981) found that very few 11-year-olds appeared to have problems with decoding. At the same time, it noted that many pupils of that age were not yet fully competent as readers. This may indicate a need to re-emphasize the importance of independent reading. Southgate *et al.* (1981) state that teachers 'Are not always fully aware of the small amount of personal reading done by certain children in their class', and the HMI (DES, 1985a) found that only in about 50% of the 8–12 schools was time specifically set aside for private reading. It found that such reading tended to take place at 'spare moments' during the day.

The problem of finding time for a range of curricular activities is a pressing one, and with the introduction of the National Curriculum there are more pressures than ever on the timetable. These various reports, however, indicate the importance in all subjects of finding class time for personal reading.

Introducing independent reading

Children's desire for books and their attitudes towards them will, of course, depend upon their previous reading experiences. The desire for a particular book may be sparked off by any number of factors. It may have been read by a popular member of the class, it may link with a TV programme, or coincide with a current interest of the pupil. Many children are quick to enthuse but can often be equally quick to lose that enthusiasm. A teacher's awareness of this often leads to the introduction of 'the right book at the right time' when encouraging independent reading. If the appearance of the book cover, its illustrations, layout, text size and spacing are attractive, the teacher's role in introducing the book can be made easier. If pupils are 'hooked' in this way it is important, in order to maintain interest, to consider ways in which further books can be put into pupils' hands. In a talk he gave to a group of teachers, Edward Blishen once gave an example of this. The school he attended as a boy prescribed a list of set books to be read and no others were to be included in the reading programme. One morning in assembly, his English teacher slipped a book into his hands that was not on this list with the suggestion that he might like to read it. The fact that this action was rather secretive, and to some extent unofficial, spurred on Blishen's reading.

Sustaining interest

Once children have the books in their hands, many will need to be encouraged continuously to read them. The nature and extent of this is likely to be influenced by the teacher's own knowledge of the books available for children. It is impossible to have read them all, but it adds interest to many books if pupils know that they have been examined by their teachers.

This encouragement will also involve ensuring a quiet atmosphere, with the minority of interruptions and without the feeling of it being a time-filling exercise. The importance of this peace and quiet is stressed by Geoffrey Thornton in commenting on the first APU Primary Survey Report, which revealed that approximately 80% of the pupils preferred reading at home to reading at school or in a library:

> The questionnaire revealed, if not an eagerness then a willingness to read for pleasure, preferably at home in the bedroom where presumably some peace and quiet might be expected. Apart from the fact that reading at home means you can read when you want, not when somebody tells you, you are also sure that nobody will ask you to read out loud or write about what you have read (DES, 1986).

This is not to imply that teachers should ignore opportunities for sharing with children their reactions to certain books. It can involve a sensitive approach, for children may not always wish to discuss what they have read with anyone. Certainly, as Thornton implies, the routine task of writing a synopsis or critique of every book read does not necessarily encourage further reading. There should, nevertheless, be opportunities for pupils to comment on their reading, which could include, from time to time, some form of writing.

In this follow-up, ways of encouraging patterns or 'strings' of further reading could be considered. A child who has enjoyed a particular book may be encouraged to ask some questions before choosing the next: Are there any other books by the same author? Are there any other books dealing with similar interests or themes? Are there any other books in the series? In this way, the reading diet can be broadened and enriched. In *A View of the Curriculum* (DES, 1980), HMI made their position clear. 'Anxiety' they said:

> is sometimes expressed that maintaining a wide curriculum in Primary schools may be possible only at the expense of the essential, elementary skills of reading, writing and mathematics. The evidence from the HMI Survey of Primary Education in England does not bear out that anxiety.

In maintaining a breadth and richness of the curriculum, to which many schools are committed, the continued development of independent reading will play an essential part.

Reading for information

> *Activities should ensure that pupils refer to information books, dictionaries, word books or simple data on computers as a matter of course. Pupils should be encouraged to formulate first the questions they need to answer by using such sources, so that they use them effectively and do not simply copy verbatim* (DES, 1988b, 16.23).

Expanding the range of reading in order to meet a growing variety of purposes is a necessary part of the reading framework. Children's own views on their reasons for reading were outlined in the second APU Primary Survey Report (DES, 1984). Many of their responses were pragmatic. They saw success in reading as a means of getting and holding a job and of gaining promotion. They also referred to the reading demands of everyday life, e.g. DIY books, guidebooks and forms. While accepting the need to cope with these and the other reading demands referred to, including the use of timetables and telephone books, many teachers have broader views of what reading for information entails.

In referring to this breadth, the House of Commons Select Committee (1986) says that:

> Primary school children must be introduced to a variety of books and overtly, to a variety of purposes for reading that are relevant to what the children are doing or are simply pleasurable, not just exercises for their own sake.

The use of the word 'overtly' is an interesting one, implying a conscious attempt by the teacher to enlarge the scope of these 'purposes' as well as to involve the pupils in an appreciation of what these purposes may be. The statement also implies that there is a need for such activities as 'study skills' to be handled in a relevant and meaningful way when related to a particular task (see Chapter 4). What is clear, however, is that reading comprehension cannot successfully be broken down into a number of sub-skills that can be fitted into a neat hierarchical structure. This is not to say that teachers can afford to ignore conscious attempts to practise such skills, for it cannot be assumed that these will be automatically acquired by children if left to themselves.

The phasing out of selection at 11+ led to a more liberal interpretation of the primary curriculum, with a resulting growth in the flexibility of timetables. This was given impetus through the general acceptance of the importance of child-centred learning, which tended to emphasize the values of experiences linked with wide-ranging activities. Terms such as 'the seamless robe of knowledge' were in common currency, and it was felt that a definition of the primary curriculum in terms of subjects was too narrow. Instead, such terms as 'aspects of the curriculum' were more generally adopted. This move away from a more tightly organized timetable resulted in the tendency to merge certain curriculum areas, including history and geography (time and place, and often termed social studies), science, and sometimes religious education. Many schools considered that suitable ways of dealing with these were through topic approaches.

Topic work

There were many ways of introducing particular topics, but these often followed an initial shared experience of a group or class. This could be a visit, a particular story, a TV programme, or any other activity that the teacher felt to be valuable and with which the children were directly involved.

This became the starting point for follow-up work in thematic ways, often branching out in many directions. In order to maintain a shape to this project, it was necessary for the teacher to keep a tight rein on it. This was accomplished through careful planning and recording, through the use of flow diagrams, and through the selection, deployment and monitoring of relevant support materials. Many projects were less well planned, and some of them involved the allocation of a theme to children who were then told to help themselves to a non-fiction book in order to work on it. This often resulted in nothing more than tracing and colouring pictures and copying text, which may or may not have been relevant to the project. It could be argued that the copying of print from a book is a necessary early stage in topic work. What gave rise to the wide criticism of this work at that time, however, was the feeling that much of this print was not understood by the child, and therefore it became nothing more than a handwriting exercise. The Bullock Committee, for example, commented that although 90% of 9-year-olds were doing topic work, much of this was 'No more than copying' (DES, 1975).

One of the difficulties faced by a number of teachers was maintaining a balance and coverage of curriculum areas. While it was important that the enthusiasm and expertise of individual teachers should influence the direction of such work, there were, in a number of cases, some important omissions. HMI noted on a number of occasions that geographical aspects tended to be neglected. In summarizing their reports on 123 primary schools, they stated that topic work:

> Often lacks coherence and a clear purpose. It should establish the specific know-ledge, concepts and skills required for later work in subjects like History and Geography and also provide a worthwhile context in which more general skills, of language for example, can be applied (DES, 1984).

Since that time, the trend towards considering the primary curriculum in terms of timetabled subjects has grown in strength. This trend is developed in the 1988 Reform Act with its designated core and foundation subjects, and its linking of these with assessment measures is likely to result in the return to more tightly organized timetables for all ages.

Whatever the effects of the Act upon cross-curricular activities and their implications for topic work, there are a number of lessons which can be learned from this work concerning the process of reading for information. These include an appreciation of the use of reference books as a source of study. This kind of reading, if it is to be successful, can involve a number of stages.

1 *Identifying the purpose.* From the beginning, the questions posed need to be real ones arising from a genuine desire to solve them and with a real purpose in view. This involves discussions in order to define and to clarify what information is needed and to decide in which form it is likely to be presented.
2 *Locating information.* One then needs to find the source of this information, using computer retrieval, library catalogues, indexes, encyclopaedias, textbooks, atlases, and newspapers or periodicals.
3 *Selection.* Once the sources are identified, it is necessary to select from them what is relevant. This process is likely to include the use of a range of skills, which could include skimming, scanning, making inferences and cross-referencing.
4 *Processing.* Once the relevant information has been acquired, it needs to be organized to meet the purposes of the enquiry and, perhaps, sorted under headings with some form of note taking.
5 *Reviewing.* The information so far retrieved has then to be reviewed through critical reading. Helen Robinson (1972) describes this as an act of discovery:

> We read serious books to get ideas; we think about them to see what these ideas mean; we study ideas and their meaning, endeavouring to make them our permanent possessions and to get ready to use them in problems of our own.

This stage of acquiring knowledge from text and making it 'our own' is at the heart of reading for information. It calls for the use of judgements, for the recognition of the distinctions between facts and opinions, for linking with previous experiences and for making cross-references to previous reading. It can involve the making of generalizations, the setting up of hypotheses and arriving at conclusions.

6 *Presentation.* The final stage involves the presentation of the 'evidence' and decisions on the ways in which this can be carried out with the audience in mind. In addition to written notes and reports, it can include the uses of diagrams, charts, tapes and cassettes, or computer print-outs.

(Further information on these stages can be found in Wray, 1982 and Northern Ireland Council for Educational Development, 1985.)

This process, then, is not a simple one, in that it brings together a number of different skills and practices. Pupils will have met most of these in their reading experiences but the process of combining and amalgamating them will need constant encouragement.

Staging points

These five stages – ranging from pre-reading to studying – provide a basic framework for reading development. Accepting the Bullock Report's statement (DES, 1975, 8.7) that 'There are no staging points to which one can attach particular ages', they can still provide a matrix which can be used to give shape and continuity to the reading process. It is possible to build on this shape, and in the remainder of this book there will be a more detailed consideration of these stages and of ways of filling in this framework and of building upon it.

3 Building on a reading framework

Reading materials

There is an enormous variety of good material available for primary children (DES, 1988b, 7.11).

[In selecting books] . . . The language used should be accessible to children but should also make demands and extend their language capabilities. In fiction, the story should be capable of interpretation at a number of different levels, so that children can return to the book time and again with renewed enjoyment in finding something new. Most important, the books selected must be those which children enjoy (DES, 1988b, 7.12).

Breadth of choice

Many adults cannot remember how they learned to read, but they can often recall their early books. The discussions in the *Times Educational Supplement* (TES) over the value of 'scheme' books as opposed to 'real' books have concentrated attention on the quality of these early reading books in schools. In the TES (22 January 1988), Cliff Moon wrote:

> During the last 20 years, Primary school teachers in this country have placed less dependence on graded readers, preferring to induct children into the joys of reading via the wealth of picture books and fiction for which we are rightly renowned. . . . Very few schools have locked up their schemes but teachers are increasingly selecting books on individual merit regardless of their source.

On the same letters page, Suzanne Tiburtis wrote:

> Not all reading scheme books are in the 'hop Dick hop'! 'hop up hop up!' mould and some offer good stories simply told in naturally harmonious language; on the other hand there are 'real books', and many are now being written for this market, where the beautiful illustrations and infantile layout may belie the extreme difficulty of the text.

These two views do not follow those of some correspondents who have unnecessarily polarized the argument. What is suggested in these letters is that many teachers wish to see a broad range of books offering a range of options on the basis that if a particular book or scheme works with children then they would want to use it. This is an issue which is pursued by Wade (1989) in *Reading for Real*.

One of the problems of selecting books or schemes from a wide range arises from the difficulty of discovering just what a child 'gets' from a book in the early stages of reading. Different people respond in different ways. Bacon (1551–1626) said that 'Some books are to be tasted, others to be swallowed, and some few to be chewed and digested.' A 'taste' for one child may be a meal for another.

Edward Blishen (1974) believes that book provision should be wide and catholic. He uses the term 'unrespectable library' and argues that no one always reads at the top of one's bent, saying that the world of books 'is a mongrel one'. He considers that the main challenge is to lead children 'from their unambitious habits of reading, or of not reading at all, to literary adventure of a better kind'. He argues that most people have a wide variety of reading interests and that without an awareness of the valleys we would never fully appreciate the peaks. Certainly, in early reading, the foothills can be very important.

The breadth of book provision is further emphasized by Frank Whitehead (1975) in *Children's Reading Interests*. He talks about the 'enormous variety which now exists of children's individual choices and preferences'. Since then, this variety has been further extended and enriched and Moon's term, a 'wealth' of books, is an appropriate one. The report of the Cox Working Group, for example, provides a list of over 200 authors whose books can be selected as a source of pleasure for children. At the same time, it suggests that this list 'is by no means comprehensive' (DES, 1988b).

It is interesting to examine how the appeal to children's reading pleasures has grown. When investigating the reading habits of children in 1940, A. J. Jenkinson found that apart from what he called 'juvenile magazines' like *Comic Cuts*, much of children's reading was of adult books, reflecting the limited choice available to them. Interestingly, when talking about older pupils, he states that 'The practice of anticipating School Certificate work in pre-School Certificate forms [i.e. in prescribed reading] is thoroughly harmful' (Jenkinson, 1940). It is not unknown today for reading choices to be limited from the early days of the secondary school by the strictures of examinations.

The variety of books to which Cox (DES, 1988b) refers reflects the growing number of authors who now write for children. This, many authors suggest, is as demanding, if not more so, than writing for adults. This wider choice is also connected with changing reading habits. Today, we are subjected to an overload of information from newsprint, Ceefax, Oracle, and professional and 'social pamphlets' – the information industry is flourishing. One of the problems is finding the time to develop the necessary skills for sorting, ordering and processing this information. It is an aspect of reading development that will need increasing attention and that is likely to make growing demands on the reading resources of schools.

Employment patterns are also changing, and there are indications that people may no longer expect to keep the same job throughout their working lives. This is likely to be the result of a more flexible attitude to work due to the changing demands of industry and commerce. Workers will need to be more adaptable and able to come to terms with different processes and styles.

Margaret Donaldson (1978) believes that the process of reading can affect the mind and develop a growing awareness 'of one's own thinking and be relevant to the development of intellectual control, with incalculable consequences for the development of the kinds of thinking which are characteristic of logic, maths and science'. One of the implications of this might be that the attitudes of mind needed to adjust successfully to new situations can be encouraged from the earliest years through flexible reading styles.

If this continued growth of the demands made upon reading is to be met, it needs to be matched with a corresponding growth of reading materials. It would then be possible to build up the formidable and justifiable lists of books and support materials needed, and schools are constantly trying to enlarge their reading resources. However, schools have budgets, and their finances are limited.

Finance

The provision of funds for the purchase of class and library books has increasingly been restricted in recent years. Many local authorities provide a capitation allowance for each school that is usually based upon the number of pupils on roll in the spring term and which can be supplemented through smaller 'library allowances'. Because local finances have been under pressure, these designated moneys have not alway kept up with the rate of inflation. Book prices have gone up, and if the school roll declines capitation funds can be quite severely affected.

As the demands of the National Curriculum work their way into the school system, there is likely to be more pressure from parents for 4-year-olds to be admitted to those schools that do not have nursery provision. This is likely to put extra pressure on capitation funds, because these younger children will need a greater variety of materials and equipment if they are going to be catered for successfully.

The effects, so far, of financial stringencies, can be seen in the ways in which increasing numbers of schools are seeking additional funding from a variety of local sources, and this has resulted in disparities of provision – including reading resources – between schools located in different areas.

As a result of the 1988 Act, all secondary and primary schools with more than 200 pupils on roll are expected to manage their own finances, and a number of LEAs are also including smaller schools. Local Management of Schools (LMS) will mean that book provision will have to compete, at school level, with a whole range of other needs, including staffing, repairs and maintenance, furniture and equipment, and running costs. It is therefore not likely that there will be extra funding for book purchases. The Bullock Report is prophetic when it said that 'We believe that books are in a particularly vulnerable position in relation to the other items covered by non-teaching expenditure' (DES, 1975). There will be a greater need than ever for careful decisions to be made on financial priorities. The introduction of a new reading 'scheme', if not phased in, could easily take a whole year's book funding. A rolling programme of allocations will be necessary, based upon a clear picture of present and envisaged future needs. This could well cover a 5-year cycle.

The provision of money for books has also to be considered in the light of growing and changing curriculum needs, many of which will be effected as Core and Foundation subjects are introduced. All this indicates the need for a well thought out and justifiable policy which will guide the selection and purchase of books.

Book selection and acquisition

A policy for book selection will need to be based upon what books and materials already exist in schools, and these will certainly need to be reviewed from time to time. This can be time-consuming, because many schools have accumulated books that for one reason or another are discarded and stored. It may be possible to find some new uses for these books, if only for their pictures. A number of schools, for example, have broken up the books that they intended to throw away into separate sections or sheets, which they have then been able to use as a resource for organized reading activities. This review will also need to take account of the physical state of the books in use, with the possibility of some weeding out. Information will also need to be gathered on any duplicate copies deployed elsewhere.

This is the first stage of the review and is only concerned with obvious gaps in book provision. Subsequently a more detailed examination will include looking at their content, layout and style (see pp. 27–8). Having decided on the gaps, the next stage in this 'housekeeping' is to consider what sorts of books and materials are available to fill these gaps and what criteria may be used in their selection.

Picture books

In an address she gave to the Library of Congress in Washington, Elaine Moss (1979) said that:

> The picture book offers the child a rare commodity: a still picture that he can look at for as long as he is able – which is often no time at all, until one has helped him to slow down his expectation for constant movement and replace it with the excitement of discovery in depth.

It is this 'discovery in depth' that follows quiet observation in which the child gets lost in the picture and wanders around inside it prompting such questions as

'What is going to happen next?', 'Where does that road lead to?' and 'What is it like on the other side of the hill?' These are all part of the anticipations and predictions which are elements of the reading process.

The growing number of picture books needs to be assessed for the ways in which they can spark off these kinds of reactions and their provision should not be limited to their uses in nursery units or reception classes, but be made available throughout a school. In this way, children can be encouraged to accept that picture books are not only for the younger members of their school and that these 'stories without words' can be enjoyed by all ages.

Information books

A consideration of pictures and illustrations will also need to be applied to information books and to fiction. Questions will need to be asked about the ways in which the illustrations supplement the text, whether they match with its 'tone' and whether they support the text or vice versa. Teachers are likely to consider the ways in which the use of illustrations can clarify the points being made in the text or whether they are distracting and confusing.

In deciding the criteria for the selection of information books, it is well to bear in mind that these books often have different purposes. In commenting on their uses, Ralph Lavender (1985) said:

> Some are browsers, some are starters, some purport to give a general survey of an area of human knowledge, some are for the identification of specimens like the 'Observer' books, some are for quick reference, some are biographies . . . some are practical guides, some are documentaries. . . . Both teachers and their children must distinguish these purposes in order to fulfill their own.

It is well to bear these purposes in mind when deciding whether a particular information book matches the approaches of the school or class with the topic at hand.

In recent years, there has been an influx of information books into schools, many of which are very attractive with colourful, inviting illustrations and pleasant layouts. In some of these, however, the text does not always give up its information easily, and many facts are not presented coherently or in understandable sequences. This causes confusion to children, particularly if the book is to be used as part of a planned investigation.

Children often have difficulty selecting appropriate books for a given task, and information books that do not follow a clear pattern make this selection process more confusing and time wasting. When acquiring information books, it is well to establish whether a particular book accomplishes what its cover promises and whether the outside of a book, together with its early pages, gives a clear and accurate indication of what it is about.

There are a number of specific questions which teachers may wish to pose and which have been produced by teachers themselves:

1 Does the title indicate the subject matter of the book?
2 Is there an index?
3 Are the correct key words in the index? – simple indexes can be confusing in more complex books where there can be a number of pages for one entry. An index which breaks down the main subject into facts is much quicker and simpler to use.
4 Is there an illustrations index?
5 Has the book got a contents page?
6 Is the depth of coverage of the subject matter suitable for the reading level? – subjects can be simplified to the point of distortion.
7 Is the book accurate?
8 Does the book present the facts as facts or does it try to disguise them in a sometimes badly written 'story'?
9 How up to date is the information? – note the difference between 'edition' and 'impression': a new edition should indicate that text and illustrations have been revised. It could mean an added chapter with the rest of the book printed from old plates. This could mean that not only is the rest of the book out of date but the final chapter may not agree with what has gone before.

The above specific questions, together with some of those that follow in later sections, were produced by working parties of teachers in the London Borough of Newham, and can be found in *Using Language in Schools* (1982).

Fiction

It is not an easy task to select books that may be classified under this heading. The large volume of books published annually for 3 to 12-year-olds presents a challenge to teachers when choosing what is best and most appropriate for their children. Their decisions are influenced by what Whitehead (1977) calls 'quality' and 'non-quality' books, something that in turn is influenced by teachers' personal attitudes – typified by teachers' reactions to the books of Enid Blyton. It is interesting to note, for example, that press coverage of the Cox Report attached significance to the omission of her name from its list of authors.

A number of teachers feel that there should be a place for Enid Blyton within the broad span of books in schools. A typical comment from one teacher was: 'I enjoyed them as a girl, they helped me to learn to read and they did me no harm.' It has been suggested that Blyton's books can give a sense of security to a child in that they develop clear and uncomplicated stories with easily understood and identifiable characters. It is said that they reinforce the 'group identity' of pupils, for the characters in her books are almost independent of adults, although adults are still there to give support when security is threatened. Perhaps the most common reason for supporting Blyton lies in the argument that many children enjoy reading her, and that this can be used as a springboard for future, more demanding reading.

A number of other books can be included in the 'Blyton syndrome', which need to be discussed when selection takes place. These discussions may well centre on the effects of such books on the attitudes of their readers. It has been suggested that too much can be made of this. For example, Hitler and Goebbels, both of whom were wide readers, did not appear to acquire any great moral values or to have been influenced by the 'good works' they read. On the other hand, it has been argued that if books do not influence attitudes, why is it felt necessary to organize 'book burning' ceremonies from time to time?

The teachers who are not unhappy about these 'non-quality' books are, of course, accomplished readers, and as children were able to undertake a breadth of subsequent reading that allowed them to put these books into perspective. However, some concern has been expressed regarding those children who may not advance beyond this stage.

The general feeling appears to be that if these books are accepted as a part of growth in reading then their presence in schools can be justified. Margaret Meek (1972) sums up this debate when she says:

> Critics will tell me if the book is important in theme, well written or not, literature or yarn, but only I, the reader, really know if it is significant for me, related to my expectation and the way I now organise in language my presentation of the world to myself (we have all had good experiences out of reading 'bad' books).

Language

Three essential aspects that must be considered when selecting books are the variety, flexibility and range of the language in which they are written. Bullock (DES, 1975) comments that literature 'brings the child into an encounter with language in its most complex and varied forms'. This is a two-way process, in that a variety of language forms can lead the way into literature.

The relevance of the language of children's books to their different ages and stages will need to be considered. Decisions on this are likely to be influenced by the possible future uses of the book. For example, is it intended to be read privately by the child or is it intended for group sharing or for sharing with a teacher? Here are some further questions which teachers have listed:

1 Can the pupil use context to help with any particular language or vocabulary difficulties?
2 Is the sentence length and structure suitable for the intended age?
3 Does the book contain too many hackneyed phrases?
4 Is the vocabulary within the pupil's range (without being too patronizing)?
5 Is the message direct and clearly stated or is it wrapped up in a lot of would-be witty verbosity so beloved of some authors who are unaccustomed to dealing with children?
6 Does the language of the book match its content?

Content

A number of books published in recent years have used the local environment of some children as their main setting. This is based upon the conviction that their reading will have more purpose if it can relate directly to the children's own day-to-day experiences within a familiar setting. This view is a valid one, but it has been noted that some children, and particularly those in the depths of 'inner cities', do not always need reminding of the life in tower blocks or in multi-occupied premises. The world is sometimes too much with them. In addition to reading about life's realities, they need the opportunity to explore different worlds through the medium of print.

While accepting the value of such sociocultural books that include the experiences of other children, of the home and of the school, there is also a need for broader categories of books for pupils. They need the 'fabulous' as well as the ordinary, they need to be taken into strange and exciting worlds, to meet threatening and frightening characters and to be returned all safe and sound. Fantasy is the raw material of imagination and its importance in a narrative framework cannot be overestimated. Barbara Hardy calls narrative 'a primary act of mind' and suggests that 'We go on oscillating between fairy tale and truth, dream and waking. Fantasy life does not come to an end at eighteen' (Meek *et al.*, 1977). The large range of narrative books that are available will need to continue to form an important part of the schools' reading resources.

As in so many areas of reading, the Bullock Report sums this up succinctly:

> Though we consider it important that much of a child's reading matter should offer contact at many points with the life he knows, we believe that true relevance lies in the way a piece of fiction engages the reader's emotional concerns (DES, 1975).

The following is a list of questions that teachers have formulated and which may be considered when determining criteria for selecting works of fiction:

---

1 Will the child want to read the book? In many situations this is the most important question. The child's immediate reaction to its 'look' will determine whether the book is taken from the shelf.
2 Is the cover attractive and clear?
3 Is the book of a manageable size?
4 Is the type-size and spacing suitable for the reading level of the child?
5 Is the layout clear, or is the type print obscured by illustrations and are the passages scattered haphazardly over the page?
6 Is the text in manageable portions, giving an impression of space on the page and inviting the reader to move on to the next page?

Values

As children listen to stories, as they take down the books from the library shelves, they may, as Graham Greene suggests in 'The Lost Childhood', be choosing their future and the values that will dominate it (DES, 1966).

In considering the range of books for active use within a school, account will need to be taken of the hidden as well as the overt 'messages' they carry through their moral and cultural standpoints. Children attending school now will be living well into the next century, and it will be about 2050 before many of them will be senior citizens – if such a category then exists – and they are likely to be faced with the challenges of an increasingly rapidly changing society.

These changes are being reflected at local levels in the transformation of relationships between schools and the communities they serve. The view of the school, responding on the one hand to the needs of its community and, on the other, in helping to identify and to articulate those needs, is one which is receiving increasing support. At one time it was generally accepted that the teaching of reading was an 'expert' task that should be left to the professionals. This is now being challenged, and more people are being invited from 'outside' to help with the process (see pp. 60–70). Schools have also increasingly come to appreciate the need to take account of children's cultural backgrounds, their interests and their attitudes when they choose reading materials.

An increasing number of local authorities have adopted community pro-grammes within which a number of schools have been designated 'community schools'. There are many more schools that are now establishing and developing links with their communities, and opening their doors and their classrooms to people whose support they welcome.

As of September 1988, as a result of the 1986 Act, governing bodies have become increasingly representative of the community, and the 1988 Act broadens this representation at the same time as giving governors considerable influence over the curriculum. In these ways the school–community links have received an official stamp of approval from national level.

As schools move increasingly towards reflecting the views of parents, com-merce and industry, many are beginning to come to terms with the challenges that arise. It is increasingly obvious in a multicultural society, for example, that the ethos of this society must influence the attitudes of the school. As Bullock states: 'The curriculum should reflect many elements of that part of his life which a child lives outside school', and, later in the same paragraph:

> No child should be expected to cast off the language and culture of the home as he crosses the school threshold, nor to live and act as though school and home represent two totally separate and different cultures which have to be kept firmly apart (DES, 1975).

Advances in communications have resulted in more immediate access to world events, and pictures of life in other countries are constantly on our screens. This awareness of a changing and shrinking world is likely to affect the kinds of reading materials we use. A major aim of the curriculum is to foster an appreciation of others and to be more sensitive to their experiences and beliefs. This 'appreciation' includes the wide spectrum of culture, age, sex, religion, race and socio-economic status.

> Failure to broaden pupils' knowledge and attitudes can lead to reactions based on ignorance or ones which assume arrogance. This is especially true where the

curriculum and reading material remain ethnocentric, out of date, or perpetuate (explicitly or implicitly) images of minority cultures which are condescending or even racist (County of Avon, 1987).

The use of books that take account of the diversity of cultures can enrich and enliven the reading curriculum and it is important that these resources are not restricted to those schools with a multicultural child population. This heightened awareness of the world around us presents challenges and opportunities for all schools. Reading materials which show ethnic minority characters in positive and respected ways are able to counter stereotyped images. This is further supported by those books that take the variety of cultures for granted and accept them as a natural part of our society. These characters need to be seen as taking a full part in the everyday lives of children and adults and sharing in common and common-place reactions. At the same time, however, there is a need for books to inform their readers, in a balanced and accurate way, of the special experiences of children with different cultures.

In this search for a balanced outlook, which encourages the acceptance of people for what they are – and not what society often thinks they are, or what they should be – we need to be aware 'of reading only those books which deal painfully with racism and the multicultural world' (County of Avon, 1987).

> Man's inhumanity to man may often be the centre of the books we read and a base for our exploration of literature and life. But if, in fiction, we only offer children the experience of prejudice and discrimination (of suffering and surviving or succumb-ing), in the context of institutional racism, then we are perpetuating a lack of balance in children's views of the world (County of Avon, 1987).

It is impossible to know the extent to which children's attitudes are conditioned by what they read, for there are so many variables. However, when selecting children's books, we need to be aware of the issues that may arise and examine ways in which their authors handle difficult or controversial subjects. Children appear to be able to take on board the violence that exists in many fantasy or fairy tales, or those stories whose settings are remote from their own daily lives. They often seem to be more frightened and upset by stories which involve domestic crises or other events to which they can relate more directly.

As teachers examine the issue of values, so they are also considering sex-role stereotyping. As one group of teachers commented:

> In recent years there has been much discussion about the way children's books shape a child's expectations of the world, and define his or her place in it. Racist content, class prejudice, as well as the preponderance of adventurous males and kitchen-bound females in children's books have all been criticised. . . . At a time when women are re-defining their roles and engaging more fully in all sections of life, children's books which reflect this change and champion it are essential.

The teachers then recorded a series of comments and questions which can be applied to cultures and values in children's books:

What is the attitude to minority groups?

1 Does the book foster sensitive awareness of all groups in our culturally diverse environment?
2 Are the cultures and histories of minority groups treated with authenticity and respect, or is there a tacit assumption that non-Western cultures can be seen as being 'backward'?
3 In what situations are minority groups placed when they appear in books?:
   • Are members of such groups shown as real, decision-making people doing meaningful things?
   • Is there a solitary 'token' black in an all white situation?
   • Is the tone patronising and paternalistic?
   • Are norms established which might limit a child's aspirations and self-concept?

They then raised a number of questions relating to other values in books:

4 How frightening is the book?
5 Does the book help the child to understand human motives or cause-and-effect?
6 Does the book rely exclusively on juvenile values?
7 Is the compassion, humour or irony genuine?
8 Are there examples of cruelty which a child may copy?
9 Could children identify too closely with the dangerous situations in which the characters in the book may be placed? With young children there can be unexpected hazards. For example, after encountering 'Peter Pan', some children were jumping off mantle pieces, so J. M. Barrie introduced the fairy dust as an essential ingredient in the recipe for flying (London Borough of Newham, 1983).

Scheme books

As has previously been noted, a great many schools continue to use basic reading schemes in one form or another, and continue to rely upon them. Investing in a reading scheme is a major financial undertaking and schools expect a return on their investment. This emphasizes the importance of making the right choice, particularly when reservations have been expressed over a number of schemes. There have been improvements in recent years, but the Bullock Report's comment still applies in many cases:

> Unfortunately all schemes have their shortcomings and the teacher often has too little time to compensate for them by giving additional attention to individual children's needs (DES, 1975).

It is clearly not possible, within a single scheme, to meet fully the differing reading needs of all children. This was particularly noticeable in many of the early schemes, some of which may still be in use. They were often criticized by teachers on the grounds that they had little relevance to the interests of children. The stories often lacked humour and zest and, when asked about these schemes in the late 1960s, a number of fourth-year junior children (year 6) were very scathing: 'It's not a story' said one; 'It's just words' said another, 'I could read the words but I couldn't make out the story because there isn't one.' A third child commented: 'The books we read when we first learned to read were not real books. The people always did good things, they were never bad.' The characters in these books were undoubtedly flat, unreal and uninteresting.

The improvements that have been noted include a much greater scope and flexibility of language use, together with the inclusion of recognizable, interesting characters and the introduction of a real sense of humour.

Many schools, however, do not accept that reading schemes should stand on their own, and one of the criteria now used for selecting schemes for supportive reading is whether they will be flexible enough to lock into the existing range of books in use. As was mentioned on p. 22, many schools view schemes as the core of their reading material, into and around which other books and resources are slotted. This can be compared to an inverted Christmas tree, with the main scheme or schemes forming the trunk. The other books are then linked to it, i.e. the lateral branches of the tree. The higher one goes up the tree, the longer and more complex are the branches, reflecting the increased choice of books as children get older. This is a model that can be matched with the practice of 'individualized reading' (Moon, 1977), which has the aim of matching an individual child with an individual book.

Everything that has previously been said in this section about book choice can be applied to reading schemes. In examining a carefully organised set of books such as those in a scheme, there are other considerations.

It was suggested that progress through a scheme can provide children with the satisfaction that comes with a feeling of accomplishment, and that parents can draw reassurance from those children whose progress appears to be satisfactory as they move through it. It is also argued that schemes provide a systematic approach to written language in which sentence length, syllables and word repetitions are carefully graded. In this way, any possible confusion arising from a variety of written styles and formats is avoided, children responding positively to familiar characters in accustomed settings.

The critics of reading schemes, if such schemes are used in isolation, argue that whereas successful readers move quickly through the range, slower children often feel inhibited by comparison and are tempted to give up the race. It is also suggested that a child's urge to move on to the next book in the series inhibits any possible pleasure that may arise from lingering on a particular volume with the desire to savour it. By the way in which they are organized, scheme books do not always lend themselves to this reflective practice. It is also said that if the story content and settings do not appeal to children, then their reading attitudes could be negatively affected if they are 'stuck with the scheme' at a crucial time. These attitudes, it is further argued, would not necessarily be encouraged if the scheme is mainly phonic-based, which could result in the use of forced and unnatural language.

It is at the language of many reading schemes where the most cogent criticisms are aimed. A variety of language styles is considered important to enable the child to cope with the more natural resilience of written language. Here it is suggested that because many schemes need to conform to a particular pattern of grading, they are unable to provide this variety, and there is a divergence between the language of many scheme books and that of children.

These are some of the questions which teachers posed in deciding on a particular reading scheme:

1 Will the scheme help to develop a child's imagination without being condescending?
2 Will the child be able to identify with the characters?
3 Are the characters like real people?
4 Is the story credible and does it match with the characters?
5 Does the story stimulate curiosity and is there mischief, humour and excitement?
6 Is the ending satisfactory for the child? (London Borough of Newham, 1983).

In some ways, the choice of an appropriate reading scheme is now less difficult, many recent publications have gone a long way towards meeting the criticisms levelled against them. In the final analysis, it is the quality of the teaching that counts, and as one 11-year-old said of his early scheme: 'I did not like the way it went on and on and repeated itself, but it was alright – and anyway I learned to read with it.' He must have had a good teacher.

Books for teachers

Over the years, most schools have built up collections of books for use by teachers, usually comprising professional books, examples of children's books, reference books and catalogues and, perhaps, stories that can be used for reading to children. As has already been said, this latter activity, while not always an easy option, is an important part of the early reading curriculum of children. This should not be a haphazard exercise, the book or story being chosen carefully. If possible, it should match the teacher's interests and enthusiasms as well as those of the pupils. It is not easy to define selection criteria, because what 'goes down well' with one class or group will not necessarily be popular with another in the same age group.

However, there is a rapidly growing number of suitable books from which to choose, as more authors write to and for children. This choice is likely to involve a consideration of the 'classics', and there are differences of opinion as to what books should be included under this heading. When asked for their thoughts on this, one group of pupils said that the classics were books which teachers read when they were young. Teachers will want to choose books for reading to children which will excite and enthuse them and which will stay with them for a long time, perhaps for the rest of their lives. If in future years they return to these books and get something new from them every time they read them, then perhaps such books can be regarded as 'classics'.

These books will normally be in narrative form, with the story and characterization built up in an incremental way. The density of their language may not be as important, because teachers may well carry children through any vocabulary or construction problems, simply through the way in which they read the stories aloud. Given a lively interpretation, it is possible to enjoy the sense, colour and tone of the story without necessarily understanding all the words used. This imaginative interpretation by the child, as in so many areas, is closely dependent upon the teacher's views and feelings about what books are appropriate for reading to children. It is upon this personal judgement that many choices will depend.

Children's writings

> Pupils' own writing – either independently written, or stories dictated by the teacher or composed in collaboration with other pupils – should form part of the resources for reading (DES, 1988b, 16.22).
>
> [Pupils] should have opportunities to create, polish and produce (individually or collaboratively, by hand or by word processor) extended written texts, appropriately laid out and illustrated (DES, 1988b, 17.41).

As the Cox Report (DES, 1988b) states, rich sources of reading may be found in the written work that children themselves produce, and a class or school review of materials needs to take account of these. The use of jumbo typewriters and, subsequently, of computer print-outs, have encouraged a 'professional finish' to what children write, and this tends to be a growing concern in many primary and secondary schools. The increased access to computers and the apparant ease with which the great majority of children manage them, are giving impetus to this development. Through the use of the keyboard and screen, pupils are able to commit themselves to composing, with the knowledge that mistakes can be wiped out, thereby leaving no record for others to judge them by. Many mature authors feel vulnerable about what they have written, and one made the comment that writing for an audience could be compared to undressing on a beach, which calls for certain skills of concealment. For many children whose writing abilities are often at an early stage of development, this feeling can be particularly sharp.

The use of computers can reduce these feelings of apprehension considerably, because the final draft can be viewed on the screen before it is committed to print. This breeds confidence and supports the feeling that through the production of their own stories in this way their own language is accepted and validated. Children are writing for real audiences with real purposes, and this encourages a sense of achievement and satisfaction when they see their material being read. Through this sense of purpose they tend to become more critical of what they and others have written and usually read it with great care. When two or more pupils work together with a common purpose, this 'group reading' is a useful way of encouraging them to discuss the language while in the process of composing. This lack of inhibition enables pupils to write about their own real interests, and the use of books to support and verify what they write is likely to be encouraged.

Many schools use computers in this way to produce newspapers, local magazines, accounts of visits, etc., and an increasing number are using them to produce more permanent, valuable reading resources for use in the classroom. The production of stories by individuals or groups of pupils for use by younger children is becoming more common and, in a number of instances, secondary pupils are using the reprographic facilities available in their schools to write stories for their 'feeder' primary schools as well as for their own first years. A number of these are finding their way on to the shelves of local branch libraries.

In making decisions about what home-produced stories should be used within the school and beyond, many teachers have found it valuable to consult the pupils themselves. Children can be trenchant critics, but they are generally fair and positive in their reactions. The use of 'editorial boards', whose membership is not confined to the older pupils, can provide a useful stimulus to purposeful reading. Some of the criteria which have been discussed in this section on book acquisition may well be used in making decisions about the future treatment of stories produced by children.

Other reading resources

A review of the print materials that can be made available to pupils will not be confined to books alone. Jill Bennett (1979) emphasizes that books are not the sole objects of reading, mentioning classroom shop packets, menus and signs, all of which 'involve encounters with the written word'. This breadth of materials will increase in scope and diversity as children's needs grow and become more demanding. Among the cheapest and more readily accessible print sources are comics, magazines and newspapers.

Comics

Comics have been criticized on the grounds of triviality and their limited scope, relying mainly on the picture strip format with a reduction and possible 'warping' of verbal content. Frank Whitehead (1977) concludes that they are 'feeble, delusive and insulting to the purchaser'. At the same time, he states that 'Comics are the most potent form of periodical reading for the majority of the age range we are concerned with' (i.e. 10- to 15-year-olds). He also finds that heavy reading of comics 'goes hand in hand with heavy book reading'.

It is possible to draw a variety of conclusions from these comments but it has been suggested by a number of writers that the undemanding nature of comics could adversely affect a pupil's approach to general reading. These are views that are not universally held and Peter Spode (1983) states that 'Today, there seems to be a more open-minded approach to comic literature; it is seen both as a cultural expression and a possible teaching resource.' He goes on to say that:

> Prejudice aside, a consideration of the intrinsic attributes of comics in terms of a child's interests reveals a constancy of style, tone and imigary . . . comics are easily identifiable with a child's view of life and often approach a child's use of language;

which, together with humour, cartoons and onomatopoeic words makes for unde-manding reading, especially as the whole story line is crisply compressed onto a single page, making the setting, theme, plot and resolution of the story structure immediately evident.

These are different views which schools will probably have considered when deciding their reading policies. Some schools do not allow comics on the grounds that if they are allowed in school they are being given a semi-official stamp of approval; others adopt a compromise when comics are used during 'wet play-times'. However, there appears to be a growing number of teachers who find comics of some value in the classroom, particularly if they are used as part of a planned teaching approach.

Newspapers and magazines

As a result of the speed with which they are produced and distributed, news-papers are the most readily accessible of all print sources and perhaps they are undervalued because of this ease of access. Their temporary nature, the ways in which they lack the robustness of books, as well as their size, may be why they are not widely used in many schools.

Although they are transitory, newspapers are contemporary, and with the breadth of interest they cover they are likely to link with many of the current interests of pupils. Their cheapness allows for cutting out and sectionalizing. They can be written on, words can be underlined and comments added, and when finished with they are easily disposable.

Newspapers present a readily available source of print, covering a diversity of styles, and which can be used in a variety of ways to support reading. They are certainly worth considering as a reading resource, as are colour supplements, magazines, travel brochures and catalogues, and the free materials that large commercial organizations often make available.

Other materials

In addition to printed materials, any review of resources will need to include the games and activities used to support and encourage reading. These are many and varied, and while some of them are useful for practising specific skills, others are a waste of time and money, e.g. those that involve repeated activities without a great deal of meaning and purpose behind them. For example, whereas matching is an important early reading skill, the kinds of games which constantly practice this as an activity in its own right and separated from the text, can often be of very little value. Many teachers of young children build up their own materials, many of which they have devised themselves.

More local authorities are now supporting induction programmes through which teachers are released from their classes during the week. This often gives them an opportunity to produce materials to support their teaching. The process of constructing such materials, perhaps through working in teacher groups, is a valuable one, because such workshop activities involve coming to terms with the underlying principles, and in this way can deepen an appreciation of reading needs and of ways in which they can be met.

It is certainly useful for children to understand the purpose behind a particular piece of equipment. Not only does this help them to handle it, but it can also lead to the kinds of discussions which focus on the reading process itself. In addition to encouraging uses of the 'language of reading', such discussions can help children towards an understanding of what the process is about. In addition to 'soft materials', there is a variety of equipment that can also be used in the direct support of the teaching and learning of reading.

Computers

When discussing children's writing as a resource for others, reference was made to the value of computers. Today, the ratio of computers to the population of the UK is greater than in any other Western country. Children are growing up with them, taking them for granted and accepting them as a normal part of life. The majority of younger people appear to be readily and easily able to absorb the handling techniques of computers and, as Adams and Jones (1983) state:

> Now, for the first time without laborious repetition, we can try out what we want to say in different ways, move paragraphs around, change and insert sentences, replace and substitute words and ideas, and still have a perfect copy for our final version.

There are, of course, obvious differences between the text displayed on a screen and that printed in a book. The screen is normally limited to 25 lines, often only about one-quarter of the capacity of a printed page. The physical appearance of a book, the opportunity to handle it and place it where you want, the ability to browse through it while turning the pages back and forth and to make side-by-side comparisons are a few of the positive values of printed texts.

With computers, 'Instead of the permanence of print the reader is confronted with a volatile, dynamic screen display in which changes to the text are so rapid that they are almost imperceptible' (NATE, 1986). The NATE booklet then continues:

> One of the distinctive features of the traditional media is the fixed position of reader and writer. Yet writing need no longer to be seen as linear, either in nature or structure, and thus, reading can become a more active process in which progress cannot be made unless hypotheses are framed and problems solved (NATE, 1986).

Because of this interactive nature of the electronic text, it presents this new range of reading conventions which, while important in their own right, can also support and enhance the more 'traditional' skills associated with printed texts.

The control that pupils are able to exercise over a computer and the commitment that they often show to the outcome of a program, combine to sharpen the purposes of their screen reading and can add a new dimension to their reactions to print. If a number of children are sharing a screen with a common purpose and with common motives, then this can become 'group reading' in its truest sense, with children helping one another, discussing words and anticipating the next 'page'.

When deciding on suitable software, it is worth considering the limitations of those programs that are concerned with teaching separate, often detached skills, many of which can be dealt with more effectively in other ways.

With the growing number of teachers now undertaking programming themselves or who are advising programmers, there is a great deal more relevant material for schools to assess and these new opportunities for reading support need to be exploited from the nursery school onwards.

Cassettes

As audio cassette recorders/players have become more affordable, they have become accepted by many schools as a necessary part of their reading resources. A number of schools have built up collections of books with matching cassettes, thus enabling children to follow the story in print and to listen to it at the same time. These can be used individually in a 'personal' way or as groups using junction boxes and earphones.

When choosing these packages, the speeds and timing of the recordings and the ways in which they match the levels of difficulty of the text, need careful consideration.

Selection processes

The breadth of choice of books, materials and equipment is continuing to grow, thus making selection increasingly difficult. In 1987, for example, 5014 children's titles were published, compared with 2934 in 1981. And the increasing range of support materials, computer programs and cassettes have added to the difficulty of choosing materials that match with children's needs, thus making it a time-consuming operation.

When making such choices, the first consideration is likely to be one of value for money – in addition to the criteria regarding content and language (see p. 27), other important aspects will be book durability, bindings, paper quality and the economics of paperbacks/hardbacks. Accepting that there is money available, and being aware of the growing demands on teachers' time, consideration needs to be given to the most successful ways in which selection can be carried out.

Although teachers need to be aware of what is between the covers of a book before their pupils read them, it is clearly impossible for every teacher to read every book, no matter how short it is. Teachers often find it difficult to read more than the bare minimum, because of other calls on their time.

Ways of choosing

County and borough librarians working in the children's service, however, whose working lives revolve around books, are between them able to read every book they receive. They have considerable expertise, and links between librarians and teachers should be developed. By working together, teachers and librarians are able to share their observations on authors, selected books and book series, together with their judgements concerning the reactions of children to them.

A number of library services also issue information sheets under such headings as 'Books to Know' and 'Books for Reading to Children', which are regularly updated. Regular visits by librarians to schools in order to talk to and with children and their parents can be a useful source of information on books.

In a number of local authorities, 'teacher panels' have been set up to help share this knowledge. Here a group of teachers meets, often over a prescribed period of time, in order to review books for their content, style, characterization, difficulty, etc. They then produce information sheets – akin to *Which?* reports – which comment on these aspects and make recommendations regarding suitable age groups, for example. These include books which are appropriate for teachers to read to children, for children reading on their own, and for shared reading or reading in pairs. In this way, a body of experience is built up upon which teachers can draw for advice on selection.

A number of schools have their own panels which assess key books and then share their observations with other members of staff. Others also involve older pupils, who are given the task of reviewing books and of recording their reactions, often in the form of computer print-outs. In a few cases, first-year secondary pupils have been encouraged to comment on books they came across in primary school, and these have been found to be most useful. Teachers are also able to try out some of the books on approval that have been received in school bookshops.

It will certainly not be possible to select all books and materials through these more direct ways. Many teachers get to know about successful books by word of mouth, and it is interesting to note how many copies of the same titles are being read in schools across a wide geographical area. Teachers can also visit exhibitions and report back to other members of staff, as well as read published book reviews in professional journals.

However, the final decision must rest with the teachers, for it is they who know their pupils best and who are aware of their interests and abilities. Prescription from outside the school will not work. In this search for children's books, perhaps Samuel Johnson's comments (as quoted in Boswell's *Life*) are worth noting: 'A man ought to read just as inclination leads him, for what he reads as a task will do him little good.'

One of our aims in choosing books and other reading materials is to encourage children, in their reading, to 'follow their inclinations' and to support them in this venture.

Book organization and deployment

Pupils should encounter an environment in which they are surrounded by books and other reading material presented in an attractive and inviting way (DES, 1988b, 16.22).

If books are considered the 'life blood' of a school, then there is a need for a system which enables them to be circulated. Such a system must be concerned with the ways in which access to books by members of the school community can be made as quickly and as easily as possible. In order to achieve this aim, there needs to be a clear policy for the organization of books and for their deployment within a school.

Organization

Many schools use some form of coding or banding in which books of similar levels of difficulty are grouped. One way of doing this is for groups of teachers to assess the interest and difficulty levels of individual books. With their particular knowledge of children, this provides the most accurate way of doing this. However, while this practice may be the most accurate, it is nevertheless very time-consuming. It is also highly unlikely that every book to be coded would be treated in this way.

Individual teachers who assess books are, from time to time, likely to need some form of external support for their judgements. This is provided by readability measures, and a number of LEAs have issued guides to help teachers in their book organization. In his scheme for individual reading, Moon (1977) believes that readability tests 'are unsuitable for low readability texts', and he bases his gradings upon observations of children's reactions to particular books. The lists he has produced – with the purpose of matching an individual child to an individual book – are popular guides for teachers undertaking book grading exercises.

Some schools believe that a banding system should apply to all books, including non-fiction, others apply it to the full range of fiction, and still others to reading schemes and their 'link books' only.

Criticisms have been levelled at traditional coding systems in that they can stratify books, thereby limiting children to one band and introducing possible 'ceiling effects' upon development. Many schools attempt to overcome this through a flexibility of choice under the guidance of teachers. It is possible, for example, for a pupil who has a particular interest to respond at a higher than expected level to a book which appeals to that interest. Through an awareness of what a book has to offer and of a knowledge of children, teachers are able to guide them across the bands. Book groupings that follow a coded system will need constant monitoring, and it is likely to be necessary to regrade individual books from time to time.

Whether or not a school uses some form of book coding, there are additional arrangements which it is likely to consider, e.g. book groupings based on a modified Dewey system, with both fiction and non-fiction books included. Other schools have evolved their own systems, often reflecting the belief that children do not see book classifications as many adults do. For example, dividing books into categories of fiction and fact is seen as purely arbitrary, and it is felt that it is not possible to grade 'meanings' clearly in this way. In the majority of schools, however, the larger and often more expensive reference books are kept together.

Deployment

Pupils and staff not only need to have a good idea of what reading resources are available and of how they are organized in the school, they also need to know where they can be found. So much time is wasted through aimless searching and every school needs a deployment policy which is reasonably straightforward and understood by everyone. Naturally, such policies depend upon the size of a school, the nature of its buildings and the extent of its reading resources.

A number of schools locate the bulk of their books and materials in a library or resources room. These include reading games, pictures and charts, as well as reprographics and hardware. This reflects the way in which books are hybridizing with other media and allows for the useful support of such activities as producing reading materials, story taping and assessing computer programs.

Another view of the library is that of a 'reading room' in which the opportunity is provided for children, teachers and parents to use books in a quiet and peaceful atmosphere.

Many of the schools which use a separate library room see it as the heart of the school and, as such, an open approach is adopted, although it may be necessary to reserve certain set times for particular groups or classes. It can be linked with classrooms through the provision of books on temporary loan, perhaps using a system of trolleys. It can also be linked with a staff library and parents' library where one exists, and it can work with the school bookshop.

Used in this way, the library can also provide support for book collections and exhibitions that may be sited at 'focal points' throughout the school. Exhibitions such as these are useful ways of taking books to children, often linking them with a particular theme established in a corner or corridor. These centres of interest can cover a breadth of topics, including seasonal ones and coverage of national or local events. In addition to the information books used in this 'mix and match', fiction and poetry books are included as ways of enhancing displays and of giving added meaning to them. To avoid the 'contempt' of familiarity, these centres of interest are changed at reasonable intervals as are their locations whenever possible.

The library can also be the source of books located in 'book corners' – areas into which children may withdraw for quiet browsing. In many schools which do not have a specially designated library room, these quiet corners have been developed, and the extensive use of corridors for book siting generally allows for quick and easy access to them.

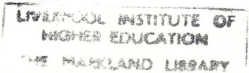

Questions regarding the location of scheme books are not always easy to resolve. If books have been coded in levels and they need to be chosen quickly – often with the teacher's guidance – it may be that they are perhaps better located in the classroom. Children, however, develop in different directions at differing speeds, and therefore within any class there will need to be an extensive range of graded or coded books. Ideally, many of these would be duplicated in other classes, but rarely are the resources available. This therefore means a certain amount of inter-class borrowing, and the consequent time lags and disruptions.

Some schools are trying to overcome this problem by using a 'book boxing' system, whereby a cross-section of books is temporarily located in a classroom. This involves pre-planning and organization by the staff and a degree of cooperation. In addition to these 'peripatetic' books, the classrooms which form the nucleus of the school need their own permanently located books to encourage a sense of book ownership and responsibility by their pupils. To help to foster this process, the great majority of nursery and infant classes, and an increasing number of juniors, have established reading areas within their rooms through the provision of carpets and pleasant furnishings. These are generally informal, welcoming places that reflect the importance attached to book use.

This attitude can be supported by establishing a positive reading atmosphere, reflecting the teacher's attitude to books. One element in this is a conscious attempt to involve books in classroom displays. It is possible to plan such displays which, from time to time, specifically centre on books as artefacts, looking at how they are made, their history and their development.

Book deployment means more than locating books throughout the school. It also covers the process of getting books into the hands of children. It involves a policy for issuing books, for monitoring their uses and for checking that they are returned to the right place. This is no easy task and, in addition to calling on pupils' help in this process, an increasing number of schools are inviting adult volunteers to help in what is a perennial exercise.

To these more routine tasks, children need to be shown the routes into the school's book collections, and then of making their choices. The Thomas Report (ILEA, 1985) remarks that: 'The process of learning to read is by no means complete unless children know how to obtain and use books. Then, on books and materials: 'The organisation of these collections is a complicated matter and the children need positively to be taught how to find their way to the books and materials that will help them' (ILEA, 1985).

4 Methods and means

The early part of this book was concerned with the establishment of a framework based upon five main aspects of the reading structure. Chapter 3 considered ways of building on this through an examination of books and materials, their methods of selection and ways in which they may be organized and deployed. This chapter is concerned with in-filling and the further development of this framework through a review of the ways in which these books and materials may be used by teachers, pupils and their families.

Reading methods and approaches

In their quest for meaning, children should be helped to become confident and resourceful in the use of a variety of reading cues. They need to be able to recognise on sight a large proportion of the words they encounter and to be able to predict meaning on the basis of phonic, idiomatic and grammatical regularities and of what makes sense in context; children should be encouraged to make informed guesses (DES, 1988b, 16.9).

In examining the range of methods in current use, the Bullock Report (DES, 1975) comments: 'There is no one method, medium, approach, device or philosophy that holds the key to the process of learning to read', and it has often been said that there are as many methods as there are children.

An awareness by teachers of the principal methods in use and of the ways in which these can be combined, and how they may interact, is nevertheless a necessary resource for teachers to call upon. They need to be aware of the most appropriate approaches to adopt in order to support the reading of individuals or groups of children. These approaches will vary from time to time and in differing circumstances, and are quite likely to encompass a combination of methods on different occasions.

Whatever method – or combination of methods – is used, it is worth recalling what the British Psychological Society (BPS, 1986) had to say in their report to the Commons Select Committee: 'Success with a problem now seems to depend more on the way the task is presented and on children's understanding of what they have to do than was previously realised.' In expanding on this observation, the BPS suggests that if children do not understand why they are asked to do something or how they are expected to carry it out, 'A task may be rapidly reduced to random guessing or undirected rote learning.'

Many teachers feel that this conclusion is self-evident, but accepting it implies the belief that children need to have a basic understanding of the reading methods being used as well as the procedures they are being asked to follow.

In *Children's Minds*, Margaret Donaldson (1978) suggests that 'A large part of the teacher's task may be to help children to achieve an efficient inner representation of the problem they are expected to tackle.' In applying this belief to the learning and teaching of reading, she continues: 'It seems to be widely believed that children must not be told the truth about the system to begin with because they could not cope with such complexities. I believe this to be quite mistaken.' She believes that, while it will take time for pupils to understand a particular methodology, 'there is no reason to suppose that children of five cannot understand a system that contains options', and suggests that a child will do this better 'if he is correctly informed about the kind of thing to expect' (Donaldson, 1978).

In addition to this understanding, the central importance of suitable reading material is now more readily accepted than even before. In an article published in *Educational Research*, Mudd (1987) suggests that 'The type of strategies used may have more to do with the nature of the text than of the subject's reading or chronological age.'

The success of reading methods, then, can be influenced by the ways in which children understand them and by the nature of the material they are asked to read. This underlines the Bullock Report's (DES, 1975) suggestion of the need for the adoption of flexible attitudes by both teachers and pupils.

The majority of early reading methods tend to be based upon two main areas. The first is concerned with turning print into sounds and then into words, and the second involves bringing meaning to print and taking meaning from it.

Alphabetic method

This was the main method of teaching reading for many decades. It depended on learning the alphabet (not a bad thing in its own right), but then the child was told to use the letters to construct a word – 'de-o-gee spells dog'. The aim of this approach was not, as is commonly believed today, to focus on the sound of a word, but rather on its shape and appearance. As Welton (1906) says: 'The letter names are names of the constituent parts of printed words, and their function is to describe in speech the appearance of a word when written or printed.' What happened, of course, was that this visual approach was translated into the phonic one and, he continued: 'It is certain that no child ever learned to read by that method: he learned in spite of it.' He did not support the belief that the alphabetic method could be used for fostering symbol–sound matching, and suggested that letter names do not describe sounds any more than the descriptions of the legs and body of a dog describe its bark. Perhaps this is the origin of the term 'barking at print'!

Phonic methods

Phonic methods are based upon the linking of sounds with letters or letter combinations through the use of 'word attack skills'. Many schools use some variety of phonics in their teaching techniques and many believe that their introduction should generally follow earlier visual and auditory training and should not coincide with the beginning stages of reading.

It is no easy task for a child to isolate a word, break it down into its components, match these up with their appropriate 'sounds' and then link them together into a unit. This task calls for the ability to keep in mind separate processes at the same time, and many teachers believe that sight recognition of whole words is more suitable for the early stages than the analytic process of phonics. Nevertheless, they feel that if children are unable to use phonics in support of their independent efforts to read, they could be placed at a disadvantage. Ideally, these should be taught as the child encounters the need for them, but this is not always possible and they are often tackled through group work.

Detailed schemes for phonic teaching exist in many schools, and can include sequences ranging from initial consonants, diagraphs, blends, letter modifiers (final 'e'), through to prefixes and suffixes. These schemes are supported by work involving selections from the many published materials on matching and orienting, and are encouraged through the use of games and activities.

Such well-organized schemes can, perhaps, encourage a sense of reassurance and progression, and the teacher may also get some satisfaction in working to a clear structure with the feeling that reading is not always an 'untidy' process. However, pupils' confidence may be diminished when they encounter the many anomalies of the phonic system when it is applied to the English language. There are so many possible variations, permutations and exceptions that they cannot all be learned as rules.

What is important in teaching phonics is to avoid using 'drills' as things to be practised in their own right. There is no evidence that skills tackled in this way are fully transferable to the main reading tasks. The use of rhymes, jingles and 'playing with words' are likely to be more fruitful.

Look and say/whole word

Another approach based upon the word as a unit is 'look and say', which follows their earlier experience of books when very young children repeat words as they are pointed out to them by their parents. This involves recognition, often depending upon remembering words by their shape, length and pattern. This calls for the visual memorizing of words, and if this is continued for too long – i.e.

as a mere memory exercise – the load often becomes too great for children. This could lead to reading becoming accepted as a passive exercise.

The remaining methods in common use are all concerned with giving meaning to print, and there are a number of closely associated – and sometimes overlapping – procedures that are less clearly defined than those so far discussed.

Language experience approaches

This term tends to be used to cover a variety of methods that are concerned, in the first instance, with drawing a range of possible meanings from print. The uncertainties are reduced by the fact that about one-quarter of the text will be taken up with high-frequency words, which the pupil is likely to have met before. As these words often appear in runs or sequences, the inferences are likely to be more accurately modified. This increases the likelihood of success in the search for context clues for anticipating and confirming meanings.

Story method

This is based on the belief that children will derive satisfaction and a feeling of success from 'reading' stories that they already know, possibly as the result of their requests for repeated readings. Children, in fact, often tell the story in the guise of reading it, which they pretend to be doing. This gives children the opportunity to bring their meanings to stories, even from their earliest days. This basic activity provides a sound foundation for later reading development.

Sentence method

This method bases its initial approach upon 'a unit of meaning', usually coinciding with a sentence or phrase and involving literal comprehension and increasingly making inferences, predicting outcomes and using language 'runs' and story lines. The method does not involve correcting every word the child reads but has the aim of encouraging 'flow'.

Breakthrough to literacy

This brings together a variety of reading strategies that have been used by an increasing number of schools for nearly 20 years, and is sufficiently well established to be considered as a method in its own right.

'Breakthrough to literacy' was one of the most successful projects of the Schools Council, where it was originally and more appropriately called 'Initial Literacy'. While 'breakthrough' is a good catchword, it does tend to imply that there is a barrier to reading and that once children have breached this they can go forward along a clear and open track. This, of course, is not the case, and as the original project title implied, it is seen, in the main, as involving children in their early days of reading.

The programme draws upon the work of Professor M. A. K. Halliday and accepts as fundamental the importance of linking children's own spoken language to their reading matter. This gives meaning and purpose to their 'writing' activities, because children use their own vocabularies and are concerned with their own interests. Discussions with teachers and with one another presents children with useful opportunities for language growth and for talking about language itself. They learn new words and structures, not as isolated units but as sequences; they begin to understand the significance of word order and that moving words around within a sentence or phrase can alter or reverse meanings. The physical handling of letters and words, which is necessary with the children's folders, appears to add to their understanding.

If breakthrough is to be successful, the teacher needs to be an 'active participant' in the process, and this involves careful planning and detailed organization. This planning by the teacher can do much to avoid the constant repetition of the same sentences, because many children need to be shown that these can be expanded or modified, and that there are ways in which it is possible to construct a variety of meanings from a small number of original words.

When used in this way, breakthrough is very demanding of teachers' time and energies. In the early days, for example, it often involves the task of copying for them the sentences which the children have constructed in their sentence makers. Many teachers have found the organizational demands to be burdensome, but they have found their own ways of overcoming them. These aspects will be further examined when the organization of reading is considered (see pp. 52–9.

Eclectic

The project team responsible for 'Breakthrough' states that there is nothing completely new in its approach (Mackay *et al.*, 1970). What Mackay *et al.* attempted was to bring together a number of good primary practices. Interestingly, a number of schools are using selected elements of the scheme – some of which they have modified – as parts of their own reading techniques.

This is an example of the eclectic approach that combines a variety of methods, one or another of which tends to be emphasized. This emphasis is changed at different times, in different circumstances and with different pupils. These procedures are common to most schools, and the decision as to the balance between the methods is dependent upon the professional judgement of the teachers concerned. This is, of course, essential to the whole process. Whatever reading methods are used, their success will be influenced by the confidence that teachers have in them. However, as Bullock said:

> The major difference between teachers lies not in their allegiance to a method, but in the quality of their relationships with children, their degree of expert knowledge and their sensitivity in matching what they do to each child's current learning needs (DES, 1975).

Listening to children read

Pupils should: read aloud to the class or teacher and talk about the books they have been reading (DES, 1988b, 16.26).

Many teachers of infant and lower junior children consider that listening to children read on a one-to-one basis is one of the most important classroom tasks that they undertake.

Teachers are constantly faced with the challenge of assessing children's progress, as well as making self-judgements on their own professional performance in relation to this. The latter is by no means an easy undertaking, because there are so many variables when dealing with human beings, and because so much that goes on in children's lives outside school can influence their achievements within it. However, if they feel their pupils have not accomplished much at the end of the day, teachers can still feel guilty, even though the children have probably learned a good deal – quantifying what they have learned is a difficult task. This may be one reason why a number of teachers regard the amount of attention they have been able to give to individual pupils as a means of judging their own professional successes. A feeling of guilt may also be sharpened if it is felt that the time devoted to listening to individuals reading was of very limited duration.

To be successful, each child is likely to need on average about 15 minutes alone with the teacher. However, this would take 7½ hours with a class of 30 children, and therefore it is clearly not practicable to hear every child read every day or indeed every week, for apart from the routines of class management there are many other curriculum demands which need to be met. The week as a 'unit of time', therefore, needs to be extended.

As time is so precious, it is necessary that a programme of individual child–teacher reading is carefully planned. This planning can do much to dispel the feeling that this is a routine and ritualistic exercise that needs to be undertaken but to which there is often not much pleasure attached.

Some practical considerations

A feeling of pleasure and purpose can be encouraged through the use of a quiet corner where the teacher and child can sit side by side and in comfort and at the same level. This is helped further if both have copies of the book. This gives the pupil a feeling of control, allowing him or her time to linger on illustrations and to turn the pages in a search for 'clues'. It also encourages a sense of ownership for the period of the reading. To add to this feeling, children should be asked to choose their own books to read to the teacher. Whatever text is chosen, it needs to be unitary, allowing for a sense of satisfaction through the experience of completing a story or a freestanding part of a story.

Once they are fairly fluent, pupils should be discouraged from pointing at each word, because this inhibits the flow of meaning, as does the placing of book marker cards underneath each line that is being read. Whenever it is necessary for the teacher to indicate a particular word, pointing a finger or pencil above the word will prevent it being masked.

The use of some of these techniques can add to the value of this book-sharing time by encouraging children to comment on their own reading and to take an active part in their own learning.

Some purposes of listening to reading

There are differing views regarding this. It is suggested, for example, that these are occasions when children can get their teacher's full attention, something that is useful to both of them. This is an important justification for the activity, but there are other purposes of equal importance to reading growth which need to be considered when planning the time. There are at least four main aspects: assessment, monitoring, diagnosis and recording.

Assessment

This includes reviewing the suitability of a book for any particular child. For example, does it meet with known interests and can its appeal be maintained through its story development? This assessment will also include judgements on the levels of difficulty within the text. Is the child able to handle the book at an 'independent level', reading it naturally and easily with about 99% accuracy of word recognition? If, on the other hand, a child reads one word in ten incorrectly, then the text is too difficult and it will only frustrate the child. In between these levels of independence and frustration, some measure of support will need to be given by the teacher if it is decided to continue with the book or story.

Monitoring

A second reason for listening to children read is to monitor their reaction to a story. This is a two-way process in which the teacher and child discuss a passage. Underlying this is a series of questions that the teacher may wish to resolve, which are likely to include the ways in which the child is using 'context clues' in anticipating what is to come and in looking backwards to confirm these conjectures. This can involve references to earlier words and phrases that are repeated in the passage and making guesses based upon the recognition of patterns of story or of language. The use of other clues can include drawing on a knowledge of phonics in order to tackle certain words; using illustrations in order to support interpretations of meaning; and using the layout of a story in order to add to its sense of meaning.

Monitoring can also include an awareness by the teacher of the ways in which pupils are listening to themselves and, perhaps, reading to themselves rather than to the teacher. It includes the use of intonation and expression and the ability to apply a sense of rhythm to what is being read.

Another aim of monitoring is to give further support to positive attitudes towards reading which can be engendered in these discussions between teacher and child. This encourages a spontaneity of reaction by the reader whose off-the-cuff comments may indicate a critical or accepting reaction to what is being read. These attitudes can encourage comments by the child on the nature of any errors they have made and, at the end of the reading, judgements on what has been read.

In monitoring children's reading, teachers build up these kind of criteria and children can be given guidelines to help them in monitoring their own reading.

Diagnosis

This is a third aspect of individual child–teacher reading, one that will present opportunities for a constant analysis by the teacher of a child's reading development.

Diagnosis includes the use of the kind of clues already mentioned but also concerns 'miscues'. The term 'miscue analysis' was coined by Goodman in 1964. It was felt that the term 'miscue' was more positive than that of 'mistake', in that it can indicate ways of dealing with any error revealed. Since Goodman's early work, a number of writers have shown interest in this procedure and an increasing number of teachers are using it.

Miscue analysis, which involves detailed attention, can be time-consuming and it is not likely to be used in full every time a teacher listens to children read. It stresses the types of errors which children make and, as Denis Vincent (1985) comments:

> A feature of the reader's search for meaning is that it is selective – it does not draw on all the resources available. Fluent reading involves the minimum use of clues. Learning to do this inevitably results in some errors, or miscues. An implication of this cue-using model was that misreading might reveal which sources or strategies a reader had not learned to use and whether he or she was overdependent upon or inclined to misapply others.

It is suggested that miscue analysis is used, on average, once a term with individual children, and that a cassette is made of each child's reading (possibly made by themselves), which can be subsequently 'processed' by their teacher. An alternative is for both the teacher and child to have a copy of a selected text upon which can be recorded miscues as the reading takes place.

In the Schools Council project *Extending Beginning Reading* (Southgate *et al.*, 1981), eight categories are mentioned under which such recording can take place:

- non-response,
- hesitation,
- repetition,
- self-correction,
- substitution,
- insertion,
- omission, and
- reversal.

To these categories, questions can be applied dealing with four aspects of reading. The first is concerned with the child's understanding of the subject matter and the semantics of the text. The second deals with the reader's understanding of word order and the ways in which words fit together and interact (this is the syntactic element). Thirdly, as part of these diagnostic techniques, teachers will wish to know about the ways in which semantic and syntactic uses can be combined by the reader in order to provide the context for the story. A fourth question seeks to discover ways in which visual perception is matched with a child's phonic knowledge.

The permutations of these questions with the relevant categories of miscues can provide a formidable checklist. Nevertheless, it can be a useful resource from which teachers may select in order to determine individual needs, and in encouraging reading fluency particular attention is likely to be given to substitutions and refusals or non-responses. This procedure can reveal something of the nature of the text itself, because fluent readers may omit or insert words which may be seen as an improvement upon the original.

Recording

An essential part of miscue analysis is to record the reactions of children to print. These records are likely to serve three purposes: (1) log the reading achievements of children, (2) indicate particular weaknesses and strengths, and (3) indicate future steps which need to be taken.

It is likely that information on attainment will be merged with the main reading record, but a teacher's log – recording the 'levels' of children's reactions to particular selected books – is worth keeping. This log can also include children's attitudes towards books which the process of monitoring may have revealed.

A most important part of any record is the personal judgement of the teacher, which may not be derived from any specific process but from the intuitive picture which has been built up through working with children in many situations. It would be useful if this part of the record also included pupils' own comments on their reading.

The recording of particular strengths and weaknesses is likely to need a more structured layout, possibly in column form in which specific miscues are recorded. The second column could indicate possible causes and, in the third, recommendations for future action. It is also likely that any original marked passages will be kept as part of this record.

Reading records and profiles will be discussed in more detail later (see pp. 81–4), but the sort of records referred to are likely to form an important part of these profiles. Teachers' observations, based upon a reasonable length of time with an individual pupil, are only likely to occur when the child is reading to the teacher. This makes these types of records of particular value, and they are likely to be at the heart of all reading profiles.

Reading in groups

There should be opportunities for individual and group reading activities, which might lead to 'performance readings' of texts of different genres, especially drama and poetry (DES, 1988b, 16.6).

Links between the individual child, the teacher and the book will continue, in one form or another, throughout school life. This is a necessary part of the reading programme but, as was noted, it is a time-demanding one for teachers. There are, of course, additional ways of encouraging reading which can be more economical of this time.

The most obvious one is for children to be grouped to enable them to undertake common tasks, with the groupings assuming different patterns according to their purposes. It could be, for example, that a number of children have revealed some specific common reading problems. A group could be formed with the aim of concentrating on these problems. The likely outcome would be that the group would get smaller as its members began to solve the problems which the group had been set up to tackle.

In addition to these more transitory groups, others would cover a range of reading experiences in which every child needs to share but which, for practical reasons, cannot be met as a full class. The numbers in each group will vary with what is expected of them, but many teachers feel that four groups is the maximum that can be properly handled and monitored at any one time. The teacher's 'handling' of these groups will range from simply acting as a catalyst to overt leadership.

Book sharing

Many teachers take what opportunities they can of encouraging children to talk about their reading matter. These often occur during time set aside for individual work and at odd minutes in the course of the day. It is often difficult to find the time to share with all children their reactions to what they are currently reading at the time when discussions can be most valuable. One partial solution is for pupils to share these reactions with one another. After their early comments on the story and its characters, pupils are likely to need guidance on ways of talking about books. They will need to start considering what they 'get' from different authors and to start putting reasons to any judgements they may make. Groupings of pupils with this purpose specifically in mind is likely to encourage a candid and critical attitude to books. At the same time, children can be informed and guided on their selections for future reading.

Pupil questioning

For this activity, a group of pupils read and discuss a text that they have been given or have chosen themselves. They then formulate a series of questions which they put to the teacher, who is expected to answer them. In answering, the teacher only uses the evidence of the text, but the aim is to illustrate to the group some of the different ways of responding, perhaps using evaluative and inferential insights as well as literal interpretations. Another group can be given the same piece to see how they react to it.

This is one of a number of generally accepted group activities aimed at encouraging ways of getting into the 'texture' of print. These are based upon views of reading as a reconstruction process involving the use of clues to form hypotheses, to speculate and to anticipate. As the reader works through the text, additional clues and further information will result in the adjustment or amendment of earlier assumptions and will inevitably lead to some suspension of judgement. Stauffer and Cramer (1968), Walker (1974) and Lunzer and Gardner (1979) have all pointed the way towards a range of group activities that will encourage this.

Group sequencing

One of the main aims of this practice is to encourage readers to follow through and to link the threads of a story in a way which can be justified by the evidence presented. It can be used by groups or by children working in pairs and can be started with children at any reading level.

Pupils are presented with a series of pictures that are out of sequence or the sections of a passage or story which have been cut up. The group's task is to arrange these into a sensible order. This will be carried out through discussions and careful reading of each segment to determine how sentences and paragraphs fit together and how they can be linked in meaning and style.

Group prediction

As its name implies this group activity is based on forecasting the next stage in a piece of writing, drawing on the information so far received. The first passage is revealed and the pupils examine it and share their speculations. Subsequent passages are revealed and the pupils' ideas are amended in the light of new information. Further predictions are made and the process continues.

This activity generally needs a teacher 'in the chair' to create conditions for reasoned discussion, but he or she must not directly influence the group's thinking. This approach can be adopted to suit children of all ages. A series of pictures such as those in a comic strip can be used, and when a story is being read to a group or class the 'What happens next?' question is a very useful one for encouraging an attitude towards reading prediction.

Beginnings and ends

This activity is very similar to group prediction but the group only receives the beginning and end of the story. The task is to decide on a satisfactory way of filling in the middle. The value of this task is increased if every group within the class works on this simultaneously, coming together towards the end of the session in order to share what they have come up with.

Group-cloze

This is based upon the closure theory, which suggests that there is a natural desire to fill empty spaces – in this case, gaps where words have been deleted from a passage. There are various patterns of deletion that can be adopted depending on the nature of the text and the experience of the pupils. Words can be deleted on a numerical basis (every fifth, seventh or tenth word, for example), or specific 'content' words (carrying the meaning of a sentence) can be deleted, or 'function' words (syntactically important).

The task of the group is to arrive at suitable words which can be used to fill the gaps. It may be that the group comes up with more appropriate words than the original, for there is no single correct answer, the main aim being to encourage discussion during which possible word inclusions are tried out and validated.

Cloze passages can be introduced orally by a teacher or fluent reader to a group of early readers with the gaps being indicated by a sound, e.g. a buzzer. Group cloze can be used for pupils of different ages and abilities and a variety of resources including newspapers, magazines, textbooks, recipes and manuals can be used in addition to story books.

Paragraphing

This term is used to describe a group activity which involves close observation of a selected text or paragraph. The group undertaking this exercise is asked to view the piece from a number of predetermined standpoints. This is, of course, one accepted approach to the study of literature, but the process can be used throughout primary and secondary schools.

Each group is given the same extract and is asked to study it with particular purposes in mind. One group, for example, might be asked to attempt to draw out any information on the author and the opinions expressed and to decide whether any conclusions have been drawn from real or imaginary 'facts'. Another group may be asked to look at the characters in the piece and to make judgements on their qualities and personalities.

It is clearly possible for teachers to draw up a 'list of observations' that each group can work on independently. Reactions can then be shared as a class with a composite picture emerging of the selected text.

Reading in pairs

From their earliest days in school, many children want to read aloud to a partner, generally a story which they 'know'. Reading in pairs can be seen as an extension of this. Children can read aloud together or they can alternate, having decided on the order they will follow. It is important that they pause at the end of a section in order to go back and talk about it, as well as to guess what happens next. They could also read a selected piece silently together and then discuss it afterwards in this way. They can use a cassette recorder and take turns at recording a story, making it available for others in the class.

Reading in pairs will call for some 'matching' of pupils by the teacher, but it can offer a range of possible permutations.

Group presentations

Reading aloud to an audience is a useful task for many pupils. It can add another dimension to print and, for those pupils undertaking it, there is a need for preparation and practice. The preparation, which can be carried out as a group, will include an understanding of the meanings and implications of the texts and the kinds of discussions referred to above under 'Paragraphing' could well be part of this process. The practice will be concerned with ways of communicating those meanings through experimenting with different ways in which the voice can be used.

A group may be given the task of preparing a reading or a number of interlinked readings for another group, for the whole class, or even perhaps for a larger audience, such as in assembly.

This list of group reading practices is by no means complete and many schools and individual classes have developed their own ways of working, often using a wide selection of apparatus and equipment. Those mentioned here can offer opportunities for developing a range of skills and can encourage attitudes to reading that are useful in supporting its development in primary and lower secondary schools.

A programme for group working

As with individual work with children, it is necessary to construct a programme into which group activities of different kinds can be fitted. Of the eight main activities mentioned, for example, it is possible to select four which are likely to involve the whole class at some stage. These may be 'clustered', and it is possible

	Activity			
	Paragraphing	*Questioning*	*Book sharing*	*Reading aloud*
Session 1	Group A	Group B	Group C	Group D
Session 2	Group B	Group C	Group D	Group A
Session 3	Group C	Group D	Group A	Group B
Session 4	Group D	Group A	Group B	Group C

to arrange a form of rotation. With four working groups (A–D) of pupils, the following programme could be arranged (see p. 55).

The next 'block' of group activities might be: sequencing; prediction and beginnings and ends; cloze; and reading in pairs. This second block in particular could be run at the same time as other curriculum activities. This arrangement would need a minimum of eight periods, and this could well be considered a full term's work as far as these types of group activities are concerned.

Planning in ways like this, together with careful attention to the management of each group, can do much to encourage all children to take some cooperative responsibility as the work develops. Critics of group working have said that groups are often made up of pupils who work as individuals and who do not generally cooperate to meet common ends. There is some substance in this, and the full involvement of all children is only likely to result from careful planning by the teacher.

Teachers reading to children

> Teachers should continue the practice of reading aloud in class; there is plenty of evidence that this simple activity can interest and enthuse. It is a valuable means of conveying the pleasure of reading and is as valid at secondary as at primary level (DES, 1988b, 16.6).

The ILEA Research and Statistics Branch produced a report entitled *The Junior School Project* (ILEA, 1986), in which it identified 12 key factors of 'effectiveness' in junior schools. Among these it mentioned the importance of teachers success-fully working and communicating with whole classes. It argued that 'A balance of teacher contacts between individuals and the whole class was more beneficial than a total emphasis on communicating with individuals (or groups) alone.' This may suggest that classwork is once more receiving increased attention, although most teachers maintain a balance between class, group and individual work. Among the most important activities which involves the whole class is teachers reading aloud.

In looking at 7- to 9-year-olds, the Schools Council team responsible for the project on *Extending Beginning Reading* (Southgate *et al.*, 1981) found that the majority of teachers spent between 1 and 2½ hours spread over three to five sessions each week reading to children. Southgate *et al.* added that:

> Teachers regarded the practice of reading aloud to children as one of the best ways of promoting their interest in books, with a view to motivate them to undertake personal reading.

These comments are as appropriate to infant and lower secondary classes as they are to the junior classes mentioned. The enterprise of class reading by teachers runs like a continuous thread through the reading programme, helping to bind it together and to give it shape.

J. Chall (1977), quoted by Southgate *et al.*, states that 'It would appear that being read to and reading on one's own are major vehicles for learning the more complex literary language needed for progress in reading as well as in language.' This view of teacher reading as a way of encouraging language growth is echoed by many writers including Aidan Chambers (1973), who says that 'Only through listening to words in print being spoken does anyone discover their colour, their life, their movement and drama.' He suggests that many people are not getting the most from their reading 'because they give little body – in terms of tone, manner, emotion, and so on – to their eye-reading; their inner ear is almost dead'.

These are a few of the many justifications for reading aloud to a class, not the least of which is the pleasure it can give to pupils and teachers alike. Because it is so important for encouraging reading growth, it cannot be thought of as a casual activity, nor is it as simple a practice as the Cox Report (DES, 1988b) states. To be successful it will need planning and preparation.

Timing

Some teachers like to round off the school day in a quiet way by reading a story to their pupils; others feel that as this is such a stimulating exercise – both for teacher and child – it is better to have 'readings' earlier in the day. Both groups feel that there should be fixed times in the day for these readings (between three and five times a week), so that they become a regular and important part of the life and routine of the class.

In addition to these programmed readings, which can last up to 30 minutes, there are also many occasions when teachers wish to catch the mood of a class and to introduce readings that will focus on and extend the aroused interests of pupils. In order to capitalize on these opportunities, teachers can use extracts from their own personal reading. In this way, enthusiasm may be sustained, and the interests of the class might be broadened and enriched. As HMI commented: 'The ability to capitalise on the unexpected and to turn it into learning which is creative and enjoyable is one of the marks of the good and confident teacher' (DES, 1985b).

Setting up

Unlike these more 'spontaneous' readings, regular sessions will demand adequate preparation if they are going to be successful, and the setting in which they take place needs to be considered.

When preparing for the public readings of his works, Dickens was meticulous. He went through every script carefully, annotating and making notes with instructions to himself on how each section should be treated. These thorough rehearsals enabled him to comment of his audiences, 'I find I have quite forgotten everything but them and the book.' He was careful in the settings he used and, for example, spent some time in making detailed plans of the reading desk he used on these occasions.

If Dickens needed to plan the presentation of what he, himself, had composed, it can be argued that arranging the settings can be of equal importance when teachers read to children. Should the readings take place in the book area, with the children sitting on the floor? Should they sit around the teacher's feet or at their own desks or tables? Should the teacher stand up or sit down and where in the classroom? These are some of the basic questions that may need to be asked about reading within the classroom.

Other suitable areas within the school may be considered – is the school library or book room appropriate and are there other areas of the school and its site that might be suitable for any 'special' readings? If there are other possible locations beyond the classroom, decisions on their use could be influenced by the nature of the reading material itself. Some texts produce a quiet contemplative and often individual response, whereas others invoke more outgoing reactions in which the class as a whole can share.

Presentation

Reading aloud to a class is not easy. All good teachers have developed the ability to listen to themselves, and objectively to view what they are saying and doing at the same time as they are continuing with the lesson. It is likely that practicing reading certain passages aloud beforehand will help to refine this teaching skill of being able to 'perform' and listen at the same time.

Chambers (1973) states that the delivery 'must be tuned to suit the kind of material chosen'. Folk tales, for example, 'benefit usually from the conversational manner, the round the fireside tale told nevertheless with careful attention paid to rhythm and phrasing pace and subtlety of vocal tone'. The reading must also be tuned to suit the class atmosphere as well as to the more obvious needs of its pupils, needs that are influenced by their age, experience and background. As Dickens said, he was able to lose himself completely in the performance of his dramatic readings and was able to follow in detail a carefully prearranged programme.

With class responsibilities, however, teachers need to be constantly aware of children's reactions through facial expressions and the many other responsive signals a class or group produce, and these are likely to influence the ways in which a reading is presented. Perhaps there should be a pause in the reading, perhaps a significant phrase needs to be re-read, or perhaps an illustration in the book needs to be shared with the class at that time. This demands certain judgement skills, because it is important not to allow the book to come between the reader and the child and some illustrations, no matter how good in themselves, may not catch the particular mood of the occasion.

Without this monitoring process, reading aloud can lose much of its value. Jones and Buttery (1970) comment that:

> If the reading remains no more than spoken print, if it fails to bring the print off the page and convert it into people and events, thought and feeling, it will do more harm than good. Reading out loud can be an oppressive exercise for all involved. The reader should see what he is reading about vividly in his imagination, for what he is

sharing with the listener is something that is alive to him. It is not easy to maintain an imaginative reading.

Unless there is this constant awareness of pupils' continuing reactions, the act of reading to them can become a negative and 'oppressive exercise' as they say.

In order further to encourage reactions from children, teachers often add bits of information to what is being read, to make it clearer or to extend and apply its meanings. If the material has been carefully chosen this should not generally be necessary, and many poems or stories should be allowed to speak for themselves. As George Sampson (1952) indicates:

> The explicatory lesson is one thing, and the presentation of a poem quite different. What pleasure would we get from a performance of the C Minor symphony if the conductor stopped the orchestra at every occurrence of the main theme to expatiate upon the wonderful significance with which Beethoven can invest a simple rhythmic phrase? . . . it is delightful to have these beauties of musical language pointed out to us; but not while we are on the emotional plane of a performance.

Discussion of a shared experience of a story is of course a valuable way of opening it up, but the timing for this will need to be judged. There are some pieces which are unlikely to evoke an immediate response from some of the pupils. If the reading touches on deep feelings, they may have no wish to discuss them, at least until they have been able to come to terms with the ideas and emotions engendered.

There are different opinions about pupils having copies of the text in front of them during a reading. This presupposes that there are enough copies for every pupil, which is not always the case, but if they are available for older pupils Chambers (1973) suggests that there are times when it is right for them to be able to follow the reading if they wish: 'This is obviously so if we are reading a text in which the language is very much more difficult than the children can yet read for themselves.' He argues that with certain pieces it is not possible for a listener fully to savour what is being read without reference to the print: 'unless everyone involved can refer back to the text this cannot be done with complete success. Usually it means the teacher is the only person who says anything.'

There are other opinions which suggest that the view of text, if not properly handled, may lead to a concentration on its techniques, which could detract from the enjoyment of a reading 'occasion'. As in so many other areas, this will depend on the teacher's judgement of the situation.

Teachers who share their own interests and enthusiasms when reading to children, make this one of the most challenging as well as one of the most enjoyable of class activities.

Sources of materials

Teachers' own interests are likely to affect their choice of reading sources as well as the ways in which they handle their reading performances.

The presentation of rhymes, short stories and prose passages can be part of a common theme, perhaps linked to class, school or national events. They can include a complete story read at one sitting, giving the satisfaction of unity and completeness. A number of stories are read as serials, which can be contained within a few episodes. Each episode needs to be chosen to allow for a sense of movement of plot and character and to finish at a point that will lead on to the next stage. It is unlikely that a story will be expected to extend beyond one term, and half a term is about the average time span for most books.

One challenge faced by many teachers in presenting texts is that of editing. This is not always easy to resolve, for it has been contended that if this is considered necessary because of language difficulties, then the story should not have been selected in the first place. On the other hand, the readability levels of many stories often vary within the same page, and the demands which they make upon children are bound to vary in intensity. If it is clear that understanding is being seriously inhibited, it will be necessary for the teacher to interpose occasionally with a sensitive interpretation.

It is possible, however, for us to take in language patterns in an imaginative way without necessarily fully understanding them cognitively. This appeal to the imagination, which is such an important part of 'storying' and is so dependent on the way the teacher presents it, can often result is overcoming cognitive problems in a way that is not easy to explain. When a class is deeply involved in a story with their teacher, there is often a shared feeling of empathy with the story, the teacher and with one another. In some way, these mutual feelings add to the common understanding of what is being read and to a sense of its enjoyment. This form of 'collective class experience', which is mentioned in the Bullock Report (DES, 1975), is one to be prized and its value 'needs to be reaffirmed'.

Reading within the community

Reading is also one of the means by which we interact with the society in which we live (DES, 1988b, 16.7).

Teachers should take account of the important link between home and school, actively encouraging parents to participate and share in their child's reading (DES, 1988b, 16.22).

Among the most significant changes in recent years, are those now taking place between schools and their communities. Reference has already been made to these movements (see p. 14), but the ways in which these liaisons are developing are mainly dependent upon the methods of organization which the schools adopt.

Many LEAs are encouraging procedures for community education based on the awareness that children's education is not exclusive to the school, and that a great deal of learning takes place before a child starts 'institutional education'. Teachers are aware of the need to build on these experiences and many are aware of the importance of keeping in touch with parents on a regular basis as their children develop. This helps to avoid the view, often held by children and their parents, that the school is a separate way of life with different attitudes and possibly with different expectations. Parents have a right to know of their children's educational growth and they, for their part, can provide insights into their own children's attitudes and development that can be helpful to teachers.

Home–school relationships

Four stages governing these relationships have been identified:

1 *Information*. Information given to parents covering school activities, in addition to what is included in the school handbook or brochure, e.g. that contained in the governors' annual report.
2 *Initiation*. Overlapping with stage 1, this is when parents are encouraged to visit the school in order to see for themselves what it is about, and to be able to understand something of its workings and organization.
3 *Interaction*. This occurs when parents take a more active part in school life, becoming more deeply involved.
4 *Consultation*. Those parents who have become more involved with the school, may well be encouraged to take part in some specific planning, either through working on school committees or, more formally, through governing bodies.

One of the most important contacts between schools and parents hinges on reading development, because schools and parents alike see this as essential to a child's educational growth. In the past, however, while sharing this view of its importance, teachers and parents did not really collaborate on ways of en-couraging reading. The teaching of reading acquired a certain mystique and there was a general feeling that this was a task that should be left to the professionals, one for which schools should have exclusive responsibility.

The close identification of support for reading lying exclusively with the school may have been a contributing factor to the findings of the APU Primary Surveys (DES, 1981). These suggested that 80% of the 11-year-old pupils interviewed preferred reading at home to reading at school, one of the possible implications being that 'school reading' and 'real reading' were seen as different activities. Nearly one-third of the pupils, for example, believed that the main purpose of reading was to meet the demands of school work. However, these attitudes are beginning to change as people become more aware of the breadth of reading needs, including the importance of reading for leisure as well as for pleasure.

These changing views may have resulted, at least in part, from a growing appreciation by schools of the importance of their involvement with parents and the community. Through these links, schools are able to draw on further support to supplement their own reading programmes. Widlake and Macleod (1984) state that:

It seems, therefore, that parents have certain advantages over a teacher when it comes to complementing the learning-to-read process. The parent/child

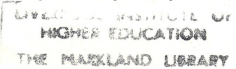

relationship and the teacher/child relationship are of a different order: parents have an intimate knowledge of the subtleties which motivate their children and are able to give them their undivided attention.

In this way, teachers are able to acquire additional perspectives on individual children that are of value in deciding on reading methods and means. In the section on group reading (see pp. 52–6), it was noted that teachers often feel unable to give sufficient individual attention to their pupils. Widlake and Macleod suggest a possible way of compensating for this.

A number of years ago, it was generally felt that parents 'helping with the reading' would not necessarily contribute to a child's reading success. This is understandable, because few schools had any experience of working with parents in what is a long-term and subtle activity. More recently, however, there have been many projects which have proved the value of including parents in some form of reading partnership.

Parental involvement in reading projects

These include the Haringey Project, which evolved from earlier work in Dagenham, and the PACT scheme (parents, children and teachers) based upon the Hackney Teachers' Centre. Many other LEAs, including Kirklees, Derbyshire, Liverpool, Newham, Norfolk, Rochdale and Coventry, have produced home/school schemes for national or local consumption. Their findings clearly indicate that parents are deeply interested in their own children's schooling and, given the right kind of support and guidance from schools, many are willing and able to make a positive and valuable contribution to reading attitudes.

Through these projects, and through many others that have not been publicized, it has been found possible to involve parents in all stages of primary education and into the secondary school. Putting aside the less obvious effects of liaison (e.g. increased parental confidence which reflects a confidence in the school itself), the basic question is whether children's reading is improved as a result of this involvement.

In 1984, Widlake and Macleod published a reading survey which covered eight schools and about 1000 pupils in Coventry. Reading is considered to be an important part of Coventry's community project, and one of the purposes of this survey was to assess the effects on schools and their pupils of joint school/parent contributions to reading. Their report concluded that 'the educational benefits of involving parents are very obvious and have been clearly demonstrated'. Further, 'a clear linear relationship was found between the amount of parental support for their children's reading and the reading scores obtained'. The authors of the report are in no doubt about the positive effects of involving parents and found that in the social priority schools reviewed, 72% of infant and 86% of junior children showed positive attitudes towards their reading and many socially disadvantaged children in these schools were doing 'at least as well' as others in more favoured areas. For those teachers involved in parent/school liaison, these findings come as no surprise.

While demonstrating their value, Widlake and Macleod (1984) also indicate that these are often long-term measures which require 'clarity about the purposes of involving parents in reading'. If these purposes are going to be met successfully, it will require the use of a variety of strategies.

Ways of developing reading within the community

There are a number of LEAs who have 'gone community' and, naturally, each has evolved a different method of approach with different priorities. Nevertheless, there are a number of organizational factors which are common to all.

These LEAs have set up a framework of support by establishing a positive community 'climate' and providing additional resources to schools. For example, parents' or community facilities have been included at the design stage of new schools, and support has been given for the growth and development of those that already exist. Home/school liaison or outreach teachers have been appointed to work within the homes as well as the schools. In a number of areas, these liaison teachers have been provided with additional books, reading materials and equipment. These are essential for community reading programmes, although their purchase is likely to put severe strain upon individual schools' resources, unless they are subsidized by the LEA. A number of schools that have been specifically designated as community schools have received financial support to acquire these basic materials. In addition, some of them have been able to appoint additional teaching and non-teaching staff.

The amount and nature of LEA support varies widely, but whatever form this takes it is the schools themselves who carry the responsibility for developing community programmes. Relationships rest upon the strengths of the personal contacts that teachers are able to initiate and develop. This is the 'interactive' stage and it is at this level that the school is likely to elicit the greatest amount of community support for reading.

Interestingly, the ILEA (1986) *Junior School Project*, when reporting on the values of parental involvement, stated that formal PTAs 'were not found to be related to effective schooling', and it suggested that 'it could be that some parents found the formal structure of such a body to be intimidating'. This tends to emphasize the importance of less institutionalized parental contacts. In whatever way these are developed, it needs to be accepted that it is a very delicate process – from the early reading stages onwards – and many schools see this as a long-term undertaking. It is also very demanding on the headteacher and his or her staff.

Family reading

Aware of these long-term implications and of the care and thought which needs to be applied to parental reading involvement, a working party of heads and teachers was established in 1987. This is part of the 'Newham Reading Programme', which is based upon its Language/Reading Centre. The group has indicated some clear guidelines for school/home reading procedures and is continuing to produce back-up resource materials for teachers, children and their families. Early on in its discussions, the working party questioned the appropriateness of the phrase 'parental involvement', because it was noted that many older brothers and sisters, grandparents and other relatives often shared reading with the younger children. The term 'family involvement' was considered to be more appropriate and was therefore adopted.

The working party accepted the importance of careful planning in a sensitive way and it noted the demands made upon staff time, the need for additional resources and the importance of an awareness of some of the practical problems that families may be faced with when tackling home reading. In order to help to solve these problems, the working party stressed that an integral part of any programme must involve regular contacts between families and schools to encourage a two-way exchange of information. It stated that:

> it is essential to ensure that all participants fully understand and agree with the programme. This is usually undertaken at meetings in school but it was considered that support material translated into various community languages and a freely available video would greatly enhance this aspect (Newham In-Service Education Centre, 1988).

This support material focuses upon three aspects of the programme, the first of which is the introductory stage where schools discuss with their families the purposes and values of any home–school reading programme. Arising from these discussions, they begin to agree on ways of making practical arrangements.

The second stage is the activity itself, and among the resources available is a *Family Reading Book*, which outlines the programme and suggests ways of organizing reading at home, including reading to and with children, listening to reading, 'storying', etc., covering a range of reading practices which families may adopt. A number of schools in many areas have produced their own booklets for parents and this is seen as one part of a broad programme in which LEAs and schools work together. The working party strongly felt that this booklet could not be used on its own and its introduction should follow meetings with families to avoid it going out 'cold'.

The third area for which materials were produced was that of teacher in-service education. This is considered to be an important part of any community reading programme, and the materials being produced provide the resources for much of the INSET work which can be either focused upon an individual school or on clusters of neighbourhood schools.

Through the work they have undertaken, the members of the working group have confirmed their belief in the importance of family reading, and at the same time have heightened the awareness of the difficulties which need to be overcome if it is to be a success. Many of these difficulties are encountered in the introductory stage, when it is necessary to consider such practical matters as guidance on how to arrange sessions at home with an emphasis upon reading enjoyment and ways in which feelings of anxiety can be dispelled when sharing a book with a child. For example, parents need to understand that insisting that a child read every word correctly before going on to the next one is likely to be more damaging than if the child did not read at all.

After considering settings and ways of encouraging positive attitudes, it is then possible to give guidance on a number of ways through which children can receive family support in reading.

Paired reading

In recent years, one of the most popular ways of giving support to a child has been through paired reading, where an adult works alongside the child. Morgan (1976) considered it useful in helping to minimize a child's reading difficulties. Its approach, however, is increasingly being used in much wider contexts.

Some teachers have found it as helpful at the beginning stages as at the 'supported reading' stages. Its advocates believe that it is a process which is quickly and easily learned by adults and children. At the same time, it provides a structure with which non-teachers can clearly identify and use as a guide to good practice. It is consistent and clearly indicates ways of dealing with mistakes. In this way, it helps to reduce the anxieties that arise from the necessity of the adult to make decisions.

Parents and teachers alike accept the process as being supplementary to the main classroom reading activities, and in no way see paired reading as cutting across or detracting from them. It is a procedure which is different from many traditional approaches and can thus present opportunities for a fresh start. Because children are encouraged to choose their own books and materials, it gives them a sense of control over their reading and it encourages them to read for the meaning rather than just for word recognition.

In these ways it is suggested that paired reading parallels the early pre-school experiences of successful readers, in which fluency is emphasized together with the use of context to help understanding. One of its unquestionable benefits is that of enabling children to spend more time on reading as individuals rather than in groups. The successful use of this time depends upon a number of measures which need to be taken by schools and families.

Introducing paired reading

Family members need to be trained in the techniques of paired reading and the ways in which they are applied. Because the choice of book is being left to the child, some problems of matching may be experienced, particularly during the early stages. However, it is suggested that adults should not decide upon the levels of difficulty of a book immediately. Topping and McKnight (1984) suggest that most children quickly become skilled at choosing books that are at a suitable level, and that this adds to their feelings of security.

Phasing

Within the paired reading process itself, two phases have been identified: simultaneous reading and, interlinked with it, independent reading.

The process begins with the parent (or family member) and child together reading the story aloud, the child attempting every word. The adult's presence gives immediate support in encouraging fluency. When an error is made, time is allowed for the child to repeat the word correctly without discussing it. If there is no response, or an incorrect one is made, the adult says the word which the child repeats, and they then continue reading together.

The second phase starts when the child feels ready to read alone but still aloud. This is indicated by a prearranged non-verbal signal which the adult immediately responds to by stopping reading aloud. This signal should not interrupt the flow of the child's reading and the adult remains silent until a mistake is made. The reader is then told the correct response, which is repeated, and they then both continue reading together as in the first phase until the child again indicates a readiness for independent reading.

One thing to watch out for is whether the child is lagging behind slightly and 'shadowing' what is being read. A sense of time is important to the success of this activity, as is the amount of time devoted to it and the frequency of the sessions. It is suggested that each session should last for no more than 20 minutes over a period of 6 weeks. If this is going to be sustained, even over a comparatively short period of time and with an agreed end date, it calls for a family commitment. This is not claimed to be a new process, but the activity contributes towards strengthening many school/family relationships with reading as the common ground, and in some areas this is seen as a comparatively new departure.

While many claim that this technique is successful, there are still some questions about it which need to be answered. For example, the length of the paired reading programme, the duration of each session and its frequency will need to be determined on an individual basis. These factors may need to be varied to meet particular home circumstances and they will make extra demands upon teachers when asked for guidance. The monitoring which this involves will also need to take account of any unfavourable effects resulting from a lack of awareness on the part of adults of ways of carrying out the programme. These are not likely to be problems that limit the overall benefits of paired reading. As Pumphrey (1986) states:

> It can be argued that 'paired reading' opens up to all children and parents the purposeful and successful time-on-task that has typically been a preserve of children of particular sections of our society. It also utilises a resource that is just beginning to be explored – systematic parental participation in their children's learning to read.

He concludes:

> At present, all teachers and parents interested in optimising their children's reading development should be aware of 'paired reading' as a technique that merits their serious consideration.

This is, of course, not the only tactic used in family reading and many other procedures have been used which have shown significant gains.

Other procedures

These methods are usually more traditional and tend to rely upon the adult, whose function is more that of a teacher. Because this implies some flexibility, it is not possible to evolve a series of sharply defined techniques. This underlines the importance of meetings between teachers and families in order to explore and understand these procedures, as well as to examine some of their underlying principles. These 'meetings' are likely to take the form of family reading workshops. They are likely to be concerned with ways of talking to, reading to, reading with and listening to children read. Book difficulty levels and content are likely to be discussed at such meetings, as will decisions regarding who chooses the book for home reading – the child, teacher or parent. These workshops will need to work out systems of jointly recording the comments of parents and teachers as well as those of the children on their own reading.

Whatever tactics are adopted, it is important that both the school and the home share a common understanding of these aims and procedures. After introducing a project for home reading, the headteacher of a junior school in Northamptonshire commented:

> My conclusions are that the risks taken in involving parents more fully in teaching and trusting them, have borne fruit in the changes in the quality of parent–child interaction. These would not have taken place I feel, had I merely encouraged parents to read to their children or to take them out on trips. By giving parents some insight, even at a simple level, into the reading process itself and by giving guidelines for helping children, parental involvement was able to occur more meaningfully with benefits for children, parents and, incidentally, the school (Friend, 1983).

One of the benefits of joint ventures which Friend is referring to, is the growth in confidence experienced by both the school and family members.

Thomas sees these relationships as important, if not more important, than the effects of these projects upon the reading itself. He states that:

> We are persuaded that enough is known already about these approaches to make desirable the extension of PACT or something like it to all schools. In doing so regard should be paid to the improvement of relations between home and school as well as the improvement in children's reading skills, for the latter may not always be as pronounced as in experimental circumstances (ILEA, 1985).

As school/family relationships grow and strengthen, the time may be ripe for those parents who are able, and who share a mutual confidence with the school, to be more actively involved in reading programmes within the school itself.

Parents in schools

There are as many ways of involving parents in school reading as there are schools. In every one of these procedures, there will be a series of variables depending on the quality of relationships, the availability of materials and the facilities which the school can offer.

Discussing the effects of parental support on reading development, Widlake and Macleod (1984) stated that:

> The schools which were doing particularly well were those which had a 'whole school' commitment to parental involvement and had elaborated their strategies to meet specific needs and cater for individual differences . . . they were not relying on a single system. Teachers were aware that one approach would not meet the needs of all parents and pupils and consequently were open, flexible and prepared to consider a variety of approaches, while at the same time having a clear concept of the message they wished to put across.

The contribution which parents can make within a school itself to its reading programme is at the heart of this 'whole school commitment'. The value of this will depend upon the school's ability to share with parents its reading aims as well as the ways in which it is attempting to meet them.

Assemblies

One of the ways in which this can be done is through parental sharing in assemblies. These assemblies sometimes include the whole school, or they are 'family assemblies' to which members of the children's families and their friends are invited, or they are assemblies for children in a particular class together with their parents.

These occasions offer useful opportunities for book displays, talking about books with parents and, perhaps, listening to parents reading their selected extracts, possibly from something which they have written themselves. Many schools which organize these kinds of assemblies stress the need for them to be kept as informal as possible, with the emphasis upon a feeling of shared enjoyment. This kind of atmosphere adds support to the belief that 'reading brings gifts and children need to experience those gifts throughout their schooling, not have them postponed until some later date' (Allen, 1988).

Parental training

In order to encourage this attitude and to help parents in the reading support they can offer, many schools now provide a variety of 'in-service' programmes of education for parents and families. They often include exhibitions that are linked with discussions on book choices, and a number of parents have found these helpful when seeking advice on what books to buy their children.

Other approaches include parents' 'reading evenings', which can include talks by teachers or outside speakers, and the showing of videos or slides followed by individual parent–teacher contacts. These occasions provide opportunities for schools to inform parents of what reading facilities are available to them. A number of schools, for example, have set up book corners specifically for parents to use for reading to their children while they are waiting to see the headteacher, or if they are attending their child's medical examination. They can also lead to the setting up of more regular reading meetings, perhaps during the daytime. Among the most popular of these meetings are reading workshops, which often begin with the construction of reading games and materials that parents are able to take home to use with their children. The planning and creation of such games can lead to a clearer understanding of what reading is about and to discussions on ways in which reading can be shared by parents and children. In these ways, it is possible to provide a foundation upon which family contributions within the school may be built.

Stages for involvement

This form of parental participation needs to develop gradually and, to be successful, needs to be rooted in mutual confidence. It usually starts when parents are invited into the classroom in order to observe its activities. This can create difficult decisions about who to invite. However, this is less of a problem with those parents who have been 'inducted' into the school through workshop sessions.

Advice will need to be given on what to look out for in a class, which as Widlake and Macleod (1984) state, should not be left to chance:

> The untrained eye does not detect the structure behind many informal learning activities. Parents will need clear instructions about the various items that make up the reading programme. . . . From these gentle beginnings parental involvement can be nurtured so that it grows from observations into participation.

In a growing number of schools this participation includes listening to children read in pairs or in groups. It can often involve just talking about books and stories, parents helping pupils to locate information as part of their topic work and, most importantly, presenting opportunities for children to talk, often at length, to a sympathetic adult.

One noticeable growth area in which parents are playing an increasingly active part is that of school bookshops. In 1983, the School Bookshop Association estimated that there were more than 8000 in the UK, and they have continued to grow since that time. Many teachers see bookshops as providing an opportunity for parents to work with and within their schools by encouraging them to choose books and by giving them status.

A report by the Parents' Centre in the London Borough of Newham (1983), included the following:

It has been suggested that all parents whose children use a school bookshop are themselves involved in some degree, whether this entails the simple provision of money for books, a regular commitment to visiting the bookshop with the child or even helping with the bookshop organisation. Most parents find themselves linked in some way.

It goes on to say that:

the primary school bookshops can provide a unique opportunity for teachers to see parents and children together in a fairly relaxed way. The bookshop creates a situation in which parent, teacher and child are often together in one place. Either through talking to the parents or simply through observing the parent–child relationships, a teacher may learn something new about his or her pupils.

These links with parents, either through home reading or school-based reading activities, can be among the most direct ways in which a school can be linked with its community.

Other community reading links

There are additional resources upon which a school may draw to strengthen these links, and an increasing number of people who live or work in the school area are being drawn into its reading programmes.

Among the most valuable of these resources are those of the school library services. In many LEAs they not only provide 'bulk loans' of fiction and non-fiction books to their schools, but wherever possible they also provide follow-up services. These can range from visits by librarians in order to talk to teachers and parents, to more elaborate programmes, which may involve visiting librarians working on a regular basis in schools alongside teachers or taking groups of pupils (or parents) and bringing their expertise and knowledge of books to bear. Such sessions are often linked with class or group visits to local library branches, with the aim of encouraging children to become regular visitors on their own initiative.

In every community there is a richness of experience; for example, there are a growing number of retired people, many of whom have the time, enthusiasm and often considerable abilities that can be of value to a school. There are many adults who have skills and broad interests which can be shared with children. A sharing of these experiences in a planned way can give additional meaning, purpose and relevance to the reading being undertaken by children at all stages.

Study skills

In an earlier section on topic work (see pp. 18–20), it was suggested that reading for information can be a demanding activity, and the six stages mentioned involve the application of a range of skills if functional reading of this kind is to be successful. Such skills will need specific attention but, if they are going to be successfully acquired, they will not be taught as 'a protracted series of practical exercises' (DES, 1975). Rather, they should be seen, wherever possible, as ways of meeting specific tasks which are real and purposeful.

The Cox Report (DES, 1988b), recommended that there should be two attainment targets in reading. The first is concerned with understanding and response, and the second with information retrieval strategies. It is significant that the NCC, in its final draft consultation document on English in primary schools, agreed to merge these two attainment targets. It felt that the division between reading for enjoyment and reading for information was an artificial one. This does not detract, however, from the need to deal with the particular challenges associated with reading for information.

Many bibliographical skills can be taught in a comparatively short time, but their applications are likely to need more sustained attention. The use of study skills can be applied to four main procedures: locating, selecting, processing and evaluating.

Locating and accessing

Pupils need to be shown where books are deployed and to understand the ways in which they are organized. These are likely to vary with location. The books within a classroom, for example, are likely to be organized differently from those in the school library or from those which are housed in 'book contact points' in corridors or corners. If books are to be accessed quickly, it is important for everyone within the school to be aware of its book deployment policies. It is also useful to develop an understanding of how books in public libraries and in commercial bookshops are displayed. An appreciation of the ways in which reading materials may be acquired from outside 'agencies', industry, tourist boards and embassies, and the ability to select what is likely to be relevant material from these sources, is a necessary location skill.

Selecting

Selection from an identified source is likely to require an awareness that book titles do not always reflect their contents, and a growing knowledge of authors' names and their specific interests is useful. It is also important to be able to use indexes, contents lists, chapter headings, glossaries and illustrations.

Having located and selected the appropriate books, the next stage is to decide on the information which is relevant to the task in hand. This involves some understanding of the ways in which the contents of books vary in their organization and presentation.

Deciding which passages are appropriate needs a further range of skills:

Skimming and scanning

Once a reader has a particular purpose in mind, skimming can be used to quickly get the general sense of the passage. In order to achieve this, the text is 'touched' upon periodically. At these points of contact, the reader is likely to pause in order to scrutinize more closely and to 'scan' the print.

These activities help to develop in pupils what may be new attitudes towards print. This is based on the appreciation that every single word does not have to be read in order to meet the needs of the reading task; nor is it always essential to read from left to right, for scanning can involve vertical as well as horizontal eye movements. Neither is it always necessary for every piece of print to be read slowly and thoroughly.

Developing speed

'Attack speed', of course, will vary with the nature of the text and task, but attention to increasing the speed of pupils' reading is a worthwhile activity as part of the process of selection. In order to encourage this, it is often necessary to consider the structure of a particular passage. The final paragraph, for example, often rehearses its main arguments and can provide a summary that can be read first. An understanding of the ways in which the text is organized can help with the selection of keywords that can quickly give its overall meaning.

These techniques, aimed at encouraging pupils to acquire the sense of a text accurately and quickly, can form part of a broader and increasingly well known strategy.

SQ3R

This formula, used by Robinson (1961), sums up the five stages of survey, question, read, recite and review. *Surveying* is a means of acquiring a general sense of the selected text in order to get a general understanding of what it is about. It involves attention to its title, to heavy print and sub-headings, to its layout, illustrations, diagrams and captions. This requires the application of skimming and scanning, and of rapid reading techniques.

Arising from this preliminary survey, there is likely to be a series of *questions* about the relevance of what is being read to the particular task being undertaken. Associated with this there will be questions, usually of a factual nature, which will need to be answered.

The next stage is *reading* the passage in full in order to attempt to answer these questions. This is a flexible stage, which is likely to lead on to further questions about the stance which the author takes up, the opinions expressed, and the distinctions between facts and opinions which may be presented as facts.

This receptive reading is followed by *reciting*. This involves going back over the piece in order to clarify what has been learned from it and to decide on its relevance to the task.

The third 'R' and the final stage is that of *reviewing*. This involves going back over the text in order to be able to apply what has been learned and to reorganize this in order to meet the particular needs of the reader.

Processing

As needs vary, so will the results of SQ3R, and other tactics will be processed and presented. These tactics will depend upon the complexity of the task, its purpose and its audience, but they are likely to include some form of note making, the use of summaries, arranging ideas in sequences, simple classifications and the construction of outlines. These frameworks should enable pupils to combine information culled from different sources.

Pupils will need to be shown how these skills can be acquired and they will need practice in their application. For example, when making notes, it is necessary to decide why they are needed. Are they needed as information summaries or are they to provide keywords which will take the reader back to the original text? Are they to include the reader's observations and comments or are they intended to perform all of these functions? A decision will need to be made in order to determine the form which the notes will take.

Whatever kinds of framework are selected, the ability of the reader to make sense of the source material and to reorganize it is a central part of the whole process. This reorganization often includes paraphrasing, but it is worth noting that there is often little value in this activity unless, as Lunzer and Gardner (1979) suggest, 'It is more succinct, i.e. a sort of precis or it is couched in language more congenial to the writer and the reader and more consistent with the context in which it is set.'

The use of appropriate quotations from primary sources is a particular processing skill and is far removed from the practice of 'copying chunks of print', a general criticism of topic work in its earlier stages. Some of the important skills needed when dealing with information from different sources include being able to make cross-references and comparisons, drawing conclusions, and making generalizations from this process of matching.

The use of computer databases provides a valuable vehicle for carrying out these sorts of skills. Computers store, search and retrieve information quickly, and if pupils are themselves involved, they will be more interested in making sense of the information they are dealing with. As the Primary English Teaching Association (1985) comments:

> Children have ready access to data which might have been difficult or impossible to locate using more conventional means. Computers offer children the power to manipulate and interrogate such data with an ease which is conducive to the development of higher order skills such as making and testing hypotheses, interpreting and analysing results, presenting the conclusions and discussing alternatives.

PETA also point out that databases enable users to define the format under which information is stored. This could have a direct bearing on note making, summarizing and classification.

Evaluating

Among the most important study skills are those which involve the reader in questioning and assessing what is being read. These call for the application of value judgements to the texts, as well as the assessment by pupils of the ways in which they themselves are processing the material. The use of these judgements involves the ability to read critically. Helen Robinson (1972) suggests that this requires:

> abilities in word-perception and comprehension, an inquiring attitude, a background of information about the topic, ability to weigh evidence while one suspends judgement, and understanding and control of one's basic attitudes.

Clearly, many of these sophisticated skills will not always be acquired easily or quickly, and they are likely to need some form of direct attention. Robinson (1964) lists 12 specific abilities that she considers essential to the critical reading element of study skills:

- forming and reacting to sensory images;
- comprehending implied ideas;
- anticipating outcomes;
- generalizing within the limits of justifiable evidence;
- making logical judgements and drawing conclusions;
- detecting propaganda;
- recognizing and discriminating between judgements, facts and inference;
- interpreting figurative and other non-literal language;
- identifying the author's bias or point of view;
- comparing and contrasting ideas;
- perceiving the relationships of time, space, sequence, cause and effect; and
- recognizing and reacting to exception, diction, satire, irony and cynicism.

Many of these skills can be developed through the use of group work-sequencing, prediction and cloze (see pp. 52–6).

Source materials for study skills

When considering the range of reading materials available to schools, it was suggested that newspapers and magazines are valuable reading resources because of their topicality and their ready availability. Their subject matter is wide-ranging from hard news to commentaries, 'human interest' stories, advertisements, and the use of a number of less obvious selling techniques. Their methods of presentation and the attitudes they reveal cover a broad spectrum and can offer rich material for critical reading, drawing on many of the abilities which Robinson (1964) lists.

The use of a straight news story, for example, can involve a number of reading activities, aimed at establishing its main idea together with a critical review of its particular purposes. Cheyney (1971) suggests that the application of the 'five w's' (or wh's) will help in a deeper understanding of the text. He suggests that a framework of five questions – who?, what?, where?, when?, why? (together with a sixth, how?) – are 'the cornerstones of newspaper writing' and can provide a direct way into a selected piece.

The why and the how are necessary evaluative questions which focus on the integrity and competence of the writer, the use made of sources and the ways in which evidence is presented. These sorts of questions, which appeal to the reader's judgements, are particularly useful when considering ways in which propaganda – through advertisements, editorials and letters – is presented.

The need to distinguish between the real and the spurious has never been greater. There is a tendency for the printed word to be too readily accepted, and although this may be changing with the increasing use of computers, Bullock's comment still generally applies:

> It is a striking feature of language in its printed form that words seem to take on an authority they much less commonly achieve in a spoken encounter, and it is one of the responsibilities of teachers to ensure that this apparent authority receives critical attention (DES, 1975).

This 'critical attention' includes using the different strategies mentioned in this section. This will provide the essential tools for teachers introducing study skills and for pupils using and applying those skills.

Assessment

> [All schools will need to] *establish a systematic approach to day-to-day assessment by the teacher* (NCC, 1989).
> *Internal assessment should be continuous, conducted through a variety of methods and contexts, and based on structured observation by the teacher* (DES, 1988b, 16.46).

The 1988 Act gave the Secretary of State the powers to specify attainment targets, programmes of study and assessment arrangements for core and foundation subjects. One result of this was the establishment of the Task Group on Assessment and Testing (TGAT) under Professor Black. Its report (DES, 1987a) clearly places the teacher in the centre of the assessment process. It states that this process should be an integral part of classroom practice and that assessment 'should be the servant not the master of the curriculum' (see also p. 81).

This role of the teacher is echoed by the Kingman Committee, which was also set up in response to the 1988 Act. Kingman states that assessment should be 'embedded' in normal classroom work and:

> The teacher's experience, knowledge and perception demands a continuing evaluation of each pupil's progress; it may be a matter of weekly, daily, hourly, even minute-by-minute judgement as to how a pupil has understood, learned from or otherwise responded to a task (DES, 1988a).

This continuous form of assessment, in which varieties of methods and contexts are used and which is based upon informed and planned teacher-observation, is also recommended by the Cox Committee (DES, 1988b) which followed Kingman. This on-going assessment will be combined with the results of externally provided tests and teachers will be able to select appropriate reading tasks from a 'bank' of activities (SATs). Teachers will also have the final responsibility for decisions about individual pupils.

There is nothing new about this, because teachers have always had this responsibility. What is new, however, is that they will be asked to moderate 'results' and, with their colleagues, to match overall classroom results with those of national measures. These procedures could well involve consideration of the effects of local socioeconomic and cultural influences on reading development. The publication of assessment information at school or class level is also likely to be a new departure for a number of schools.

In order to help to clarify these processes, the Secretary of State agreed that there should be a new description for year groups. This was proposed by the National Curriculum Council (1989) and included the following designations:

- 'R' for the majority of pupils aged 4–5;
- 'Y1' for the majority of pupils aged 5–6;
- 'Y2' for the majority of pupils aged 6–7;
- 'Y3' for the majority of pupils aged 7–8;
- . . . . ;
- 'Y13' for the majority of pupils aged 17–18.

There is, then, a clear need to examine the rationale upon which teachers' assessment procedures are built, and which they can use as support when making their judgements on reading attainments.

This rationale can be based upon the resolution of a number of questions. The first of these is very basic and is concerned with what a teacher needs to assess in children's reading growth. The second series of questions is aimed at examining problems which are common to this assessment process. It is then necessary to consider the variety of procedures which can be used to resolve these sets of questions.

What needs to be assessed?

1 How can children's reading materials be matched to their needs, abilities and interests? Children are not always working with books and materials that are appropriate. The 'interest' levels of texts together with their 'technical' levels, including language structure and specific vocabulary, need to be reviewed constantly if a reasonable match is to be achieved.

2 How are pupils progressing in their reading? This is, of course, the basic question constantly being asked by teachers, and is one of the main concerns of parents and governors, and of the children themselves. It involves making

comparisons with past achievements and predictions about future reading development. This then leads on to two further basic questions.

3 What problems or difficulties are individual children meeting which inhibit the growth of their reading?

4 How do children in a particular group or class compare with the broad range of others in similar age groups and are they meeting the 'standards' of their peers?

These are the kinds of questions which are readily asked by the public and the media but which, for reading at least, cannot always be answered in a simple way.

Problems of assessment

The first and most obvious problem with assessment lies in the nature of reading itself. If it were no more than the matching of appropriate sounds to their letters, then reading could be tested quickly and efficiently by using the many phonic measures available. However, these measures only deal with one particular aspect of reading, and they are not designed to measure the broader functions of reading. It is less easy to assess the processes of thinking, feeling and imagining, which the reading act demands. It is possible to arrive at some indication of how a text may affect a pupil's thinking, but the assessment of personal responses is a more difficult task.

A second problem arises because of the lack of agreement over the meaning of terms used in assessment. Before the TGAT report (DES, 1987a) was produced, many commentators on the Education Act appeared to confuse diagnostic measures with those of assessment. Other terms like 'screening', 'monitoring', 'testing' and 'evaluating' were often used loosely, which tended to add to the confusion.

A third problem concerns reading ages. These are considered by Bullock (DES, 1975) to be based upon 'a misleading concept which can obscure more than it reveals'. Reading ages are often determined through the submission of word recognition tests, which use words in isolation and, as such, do not necessarily measure a child's ability to read fluently and with understanding. The ability to extract meanings through the interrelationships of words and through anticipating language patterns is not needed when dealing with these kinds of tests.

Those measures which do use 'units of meaning', such as sentence completion tests, can also be of limited value. In a number of examples, it is possible for a good reader, when filling the gaps, to justify the selection of a number of words from those listed that might be entirely appropriate to the meaning of the sentence. If the words selected are not those envisaged by the authors of the tests, lower marks can be accorded, even though the reader is coping effectively with the questions.

These kinds of problems associated with standardized testing, together with the ways in which 'results' – often recorded in numerical form – are misinterpreted by the public, have tended to focus the critical attention of teachers upon measures currently available. Many teachers are unhappy about them and are seeking ways in which more relevant procedures may be used.

In this search, there is concern over the amount of class time that many assessment procedures demand. With some, it is all too easy to spend time testing and not teaching, thereby resulting in a 'paralysis through analysis'. There is clearly an articulated desire for test measures which can be used as teaching instruments.

Assessment methods and procedures

Of its four main criteria, TGAT (DES, 1987a) states that assessment should be 'formative', in that it should provide information for future teaching approaches and form a basis for class and individual planning. This implies the use of a variety of assessment procedures with a clear understanding of the purposes of each.

Levels of text difficulty

In order to match a pupil with print successfully, it is necessary to be aware of the 'difficulty levels' of the particular text. This can involve the application of a range of readability measures. Many of these use formulae based upon the belief that combinations of word and sentence lengths can give reasonably good predictions of text difficulty. Among the better known are the Mufgord Readability Chart, the Flesch Formula and the Fog Index, and a number of schools are making increasing use of computers in deciding on the difficulty levels of texts. The application of cloze procedures have also been found helpful.

All of these procedures can provide useful guides for teachers, but the most successful ways of determining readability levels are those based upon the judgements made by small groups of teachers, who are able to assess the material in the light of their knowledge of their pupils. These review procedures occasionally reveal disparities between what authors feel are suitable for particular age groups and the views of teachers.

Although such group decisions on readability are most valuable, they are also time-consuming and it is certainly not possible to apply them to every book. As their knowledge of books grows with the introduction of new publications, many teachers build up their own checklists which they use in determining the suitability of books for particular children. Adams and Jones (1983) suggest that 'By far the most accurate means yet available to us of assessing readability is to use a computer programme.' They continue:

> If such programmes are sensitively employed (which means with a writer's and teacher's eye and instinct and not in a purely mechanistic way) we should be able to improve considerably our judgement about the text which we present to students.

Informal ways of monitoring reading progress

When a child is working on a text, there are a number of procedures that teachers can use in broadening their knowledge of reading progress. One of the most common of these procedures is monitoring, which may involve regular spot-checks on children's reactions to books as the teacher walks around the classroom. Used in this way, only a few minutes of the teacher's time is likely to be taken up. Questions may also be asked relating to the illustrations, story development and characters. At periodic intervals, this procedure can be enhanced with more comprehensive monitoring, e.g. when a child has completed a book or reached a significant stage in a story. At this point, more detailed discussions can take place between the teacher and pupil, who together can begin to share critical insights into what is read.

In these ways, teachers are able to build up quite detailed pictures of their pupils' reading development.

Screening and diagnosing

In addition to these less formal monitoring procedures, teachers are likely to apply more specific measures from time to time, e.g. the use of screening procedures to identify children who are experiencing reading difficulties as well as those who are likely to present future problems. The term 'screening' implies the application of a variety of techniques as a mesh or sieve which teachers can vary in 'size' according to the purpose they have in mind. There are a number of tests available, among which the Aston Index (Newton and Thomson, 1976) is probably most widely known. Many LEAs use some variety of screening procedures which focus on reading skills appropriate to the age groups being tested.

Once screening procedures have identified those who have not reached a satisfactory level of performance, the next stage involves a closer look at these pupils. This attempts to discover the sources of their difficulties with a view to planning treatment.

This process of diagnosis can be a broad one, ranging from an examination of word attack and phonic skills through to a more comprehensive study of any underlying cognitive weaknesses. To meet the specific needs of individual children revealed through screening, there is a great variety of diagnostic measures which teachers can use and adapt to meet their needs (see Vincent, 1985). Readability measures, monitoring (see pp. 49–51), screening and diagnosing all form part of the resources used to meet these needs, and they are an essential part of the overall evaluation of reading progress. Much of this evaluation will, however, be concerned with assessment that can be considered in terms of 'test' or 'non-test' procedures.

Testing and non-testing

Until recently, tests tended to be mainly normative – based upon a standard, an average or a 'norm' – and used as a yardstick against which groups or individual children could be compared. In order to arrive at a norm within a particular test, trials were carried out with children covering a wide range of abilities.

In a 'normal' group, about half of the pupils in such a test would be below its average and the remainder above. It can therefore be damaging if those pupils who are below average in such tests are regarded as failures. Standardized normative tests are designed to cover the whole spread of ability and if, within a school, half of the children tested are below average, then this can only reflect the national position.

The possible misinterpretation of external normative tests is one of the reasons why TGAT and the Cox Working Group do not support their use in school. The TGAT report (DES, 1987a) asserts that such tests 'are not usually related, in either construction or subsequent use to the normal work of teachers'. It continues: 'The resources devoted to such testing have been scarcely justified, and the more limited types of test have themselves given testing in general a reputation for narrowness and irrelevance.'

While rejecting such normative tests, the report is clear in its support of those measures which are concerned with the success of pupils in meeting specific targets which have been set for them. It suggests that the use of such 'target testing' or criterion-referenced procedures can help to inform teachers' judgements. These, it states, are needed in order to achieve formative assessment as well as playing an important part in 'the dissemination of a shared language for discussing attainment at all levels – the central function of attainment'. The values of this 'shared language', through which teachers are able to agree on a vocabulary of assessment, will be particularly significant when moderating procedures are applied.

A number of teachers have designed their own criterion-referenced tests, which are related to their own class reading programmes. While much of the work of the APU points towards the production of target tests which are linked with good classroom practices, there are at the moment few such tests generally available. It is anticipated that the Standardized Assessment Tasks (SATs) being worked out by the various consortia through the School Examinations and Assessment Council will result in many more becoming accessible to teachers.

There are, however, many examples of the second main element of assessment – non-test procedures. These depend upon the expert observations of teachers, which 'cannot be valued too highly' (DES, 1975). This comment is reflected in the report of the Cox Working Group (DES, 1988b), which recommends that 'the bulk of the assessment should be internal and continuous based upon structured observation by the teacher'.

As part of their observation framework, teachers can build up a series of checklists, notes, outlines or flow diagrams that will focus on different aspects of children's reading, e.g. pupils' approaches to books, their voluntary reading habits, their attitudes to books and the ways in which they respond to reading by the teacher. A valuable dimension to these non-test procedures is one in which children's comments on their own reading are considered. Children are often clear about how their reading is developing, and opportunities to discuss this with their teacher not only helps in the assessment process but also gives impetus and interest to that development.

This framework can be further extended through an examination of the ways in which pupils undertake different reading tasks. These are likely to include such activities as reading to follow a sequence of instructions, reading to gain an overall impression of a text and reading to expand on information, and many of the reading demands referred to in the section on study skills (see pp. 70–5) can form part of this checklist.

The ways in which children read aloud – their word attack, word recognition and reading rates – can all be included, and the processes which were considered in the sections on listening to children read (pp. 48–51) and group working (pp. 52–6) are likely to provide useful material for inclusion in the assessment framework. In particular, the use of miscue analysis, specifically mentioned in both the Cox Reports (1988b, 1989b), can form the core of any internal assessment procedure.

This series of processes can provide what TGAT (DES, 1987a) calls 'A variety of methods of exploring and assessing pupils' responses', which teachers may use as a guide when developing their own performance ratings of pupils, and through which the assessment process is 'an integral part of the Educational process continually providing both "feedback" and "feed forward"'.

Recording reading development

> *The record of the continuous assessment should cover what the child has read; the child's reading strategies and approaches when handling familiar text, levels of comprehension; retrieval of information; and the child's reading tastes and preferences* (DES, 1988b, 16.48).

The recommendations of the Black Report (DES, 1987a) stress the use of assessment procedures based upon day-to-day class activities. This is supported by the Cox Report (DES, 1988b), which refers to this ongoing process as using a variety of methods and in a variety of contexts. Both these reports, together with that of the Kingman Inquiry, underline the importance of the role of teachers in keeping cumulative records from a child's earliest days in school. Such records will need to reflect the breadth of these processes of assessment.

It has been suggested that the School Examination and Assessment Council will develop a format that will be standardized and used nationally for recording children's language development. This may be based upon the *Primary Language Record* (ILEA, 1988a), the type of record which the Cox Report commends. It includes space for recording parental comments, and children will also be 'actively involved in the evaluation of their own progress and the planning of their work'. These records are also designed to involve all teachers who teach the child, including any support teachers working in the school. If a National Language Record is produced, although this is by no means certain it will need to be backed-up by teachers' own personal diaries or logs which, when periodically reviewed, present a valuable picture of the reading development of individual children.

From time to time, all of this information will need to be assessed, summarized and shaped. This processing is likely to be aimed at building up a class reading record. In determining its content and format, the following questions will need to be considered:

- How long will the records take to compile?
- To what use will they be put?
- What values will they have for children's future teachers?
- What are the details that need to be recorded?
- To what extent can children's comments on their own reading be included?
- Should there be a place for recording the observations of parents?
- To what extent will the records be cumulative?
- Within the National Curriculum, how will reading records match with the attainment targets, each with their five levels?

Any reading record should have at its core at least five main sections:

1 A representative list of books read by children, together with their levels (independent, instruction, frustration).
2 Details of specific strengths.
3 Details of particular weaknesses.
4 An outline of future plans being developed by the teacher.
5 A section reserved for a commentary.

A number of teachers now use computers to compile their reading records. These may well help alleviate the time problem associated with the recording process, which makes such heavy demands on teachers.

Transfer between schools

The attainment targets and programmes of study for English will provide a firmer basis than ever before for liaison between schools. Within the framework provided by our report teachers will be able to ensure for their pupils a curriculum which has shape and sequence and which is mutually understood, thereby providing a sense of continuity and progression as pupils move from one phase of schooling to another (DES, 1988b, 3.2).

The use of accurate, relevant and 'formative' reading records is particularly important at the points of transfer between stages of education. At these significant times in a child's life, reading attainment is seen as exerting a major influence upon success or failure when entering the next phase. Children's reading grows incrementally with their broadening experiences and, if this process is not to be checked at transfer, there need to be agreed procedures to support and maintain its continuity. The concept of 'levels' assumes:

that all or virtually all children will travel along broadly the same curriculum path in English, but that some will move more quickly, and further than others; and some may hover around the level 1 attainments for the whole of their school careers (DES, 1988b).

These levels, then, will cut across age ranges, e.g. level 5 is likely to apply to many children in the early years of secondary schooling as well as to a number at the primary stage. Similarly, level 3 will apply to some infant as well as to some junior children. The successful implementation of attainment targets, programmes of study and assessment measures will need close and continuous cooperation between all stages.

Infant–junior transfer

As part of the *Newham Reading Programme* (Newham In-Service Education Centre, 1988), a working group of primary headteachers focused upon transfer at 7 years. Although many infant and junior schools are sited close to one another, with some sharing the same building complex, it was felt by the Newham group that this closeness is not always reflected in the continuity of reading development which schools would like to see. It was also felt that even in some primary schools (5- to 11-year-olds) reading growth sometimes suffers as a result of the transfer between the infant and junior stages.

In facing this problem, the Newham group made a number of recommendations aimed at encouraging a greater understanding by teachers of the professional demands made upon their colleagues:

1 That courses on classroom management of the language curriculum be mounted.
2 That a training day be set aside for the staffs of infant and junior schools jointly to develop reading procedures.
3 That a cumulative record of children's achievement be produced.
4 That, as far as possible, first year junior classes should be taught by experienced teachers.
5 That in order to meet the needs of informed adults working within classrooms, a training scheme be established for additional welfare assistants to support class teachers in reading development.
6 That infant and matching junior schools should attempt to plan together a joint reading programme.
7 That, wherever possible, infant and junior schools should establish a joint reading resource area/room.
8 That a teacher appointment (without classroom responsibility) be made for infant and their junior schools which must not be seen in terms of a remedial or supply post, but to assist in the development of the Newham Reading Programme throughout the schools.

While accepting the financial constraints imposed by LMS and the possible limitations of the 'poll tax', the Newham group felt it necessary to point out that a number of their recommendations called for some additional funding. At the same time, it made a number of suggestions which have no direct financial implications. These include teacher exchanges, the joint use of reading materials and an increased understanding of ways in which they are applied.

In the planning of a joint reading programme, the Newham group took account of the Bullock Report: 'It must be emphasised that continuity in respect of language and reading needs must receive detailed attention in its own right' (DES, 1975). It went on to identify a number of key aspects of such a joint programme.

It was noted that in some cases, different interpretations of colour-coded book 'levels' existed between infant and junior schools, and it was felt that, in order to overcome any disparity, both colour-coding systems should be recorded and made available to each school. Other aspects that the Newham group felt needed common attention included reading methods and approaches, class and school organization, assessment procedures, monitoring, recording and profiling, and shared approaches to family involvement.

The Newham group then considered broader issues of transfer, which may apply to any stage and which could provide a predictable background against which reading growth needs to be set:

1 *The curriculum* – with possible different ways of interpreting it through changing organizations and different teaching styles and expectations.
2 *Social aspects* – reflecting changes in friendship patterns and peer groups following transfer to larger schools. Most noticeable here are the changes which pupils experience from being 'top of the pile' in one school to becoming very junior members of the next. This involves a transfer of fidelity, which may also be reflected in the extent and nature of parental involvement with the child's 'new' school.
3 *Environmental change* – for many pupils this involves working in a much larger school, often of a different design and with different expectations, and calling for considerable readjustment.

The heads in the group felt that many children see these changes as exciting and offering them a new start. In order not to inhibit these feelings, it was felt that reading records should be carefully produced and that personal contacts between teachers in receiving and 'feeder' schools were essential if these records were to be meaningful.

Primary–secondary transfer

In a report on secondary transfer, ILEA (1988b) states that 'Most 11 year olds settle down at secondary school better than their primary teachers might have predicted.' At the same time, the report notes the 'major influence exerted by reading attainment on children's success at secondary level'.

Reading is a key factor in the transfer process, particularly for those pupils who have reading difficulties. ILEA (1988b) states that 'on the evidence we have found, there is a very strong case for early identification of reading difficulties and for pushing resources back down the ladder into the primary school'. This is one of the clearest statements yet on the importance of additional resources for younger children on the grounds that preventative measures are better than curative ones.

The sharing of resources in this way can establish a firm foundation for many other liaison activities, for resources alone are not sufficient. These activities often include common approaches to the use of materials and to their organization, something that is now actively engaging many teachers at both the primary and secondary levels. They also include exchange visits of teachers and pupils, joint policy meetings on such aspects of reading as assessment and recording, older pupils working alongside and helping younger children, and classes of fourth-year juniors (year 6) working for short periods in their future secondary schools. A number of secondary schools deliberately organize their first years on primary lines, matching the approaches of their feeder schools. These arrangements often include a more general first-year course, with teachers having much more contact time with their pupils.

There are as many different procedures as there are schools, but if reading development is to receive the support and encouragement which successive reports from Bullock to Cox have advocated, then these liaison procedures will need to be encouraged and nurtured further.

Reading co-ordinators

Primary schools must have a clear policy and whole school approach to the teaching of reading (DES, 1988b, 3.10).

Schools must provide a dynamic reading environment where children are motivated to take their place as readers, encouraged and supported by structured and sensitive teaching (DES, 1988b, 3.10).

The key figures in the liaison process are likely to be those teachers who have specific responsibilities for reading development within schools. While it is accepted that 'every teacher is a teacher of reading', there are additional responsibilities for those members of staff who have been designated as 'co-ordinators' or 'consultants'.

From the Plowden Report (DES, 1966) onwards, support has been given to the establishment of 'graded posts', and schools have responded by developing such posts. The white paper on *Teaching Quality* (DES, 1983b) said that 'The government believes that all primary teachers should be equipped to take a particular responsibility for one aspect of the curriculum.' This implies that a designated responsibility would not necessarily bring with it an incentive allowance. The decision of the 1988 Act to include English as one of the core subjects, and the centrality of reading to all of the above, nevertheless emphasizes the need for the establishment of a senior post for reading/language development in all schools. For example, the Kingman Report (DES, 1988a) recommends that 'All primary schools should have a member of staff who is designated as a language consultant, and who has the responsibility for advising on and co-ordinating language work.' These broad terms of reference are similar to what language co-ordinators are already doing in many schools.

Nevertheless, there are a number of problems that consultant teachers need to overcome if they are going to undertake their co-ordinating functions successfully.

Some problems raised by language co-ordinators

In primary or middle schools, teachers with specific curriculum responsibilities are usually also full-time class teachers. This one teacher one class situation, which is considered to be of such importance to the accepted primary approach, does not readily lend itself to 'specialism'. Because their priorities lie with their own class, teachers often find it difficult to make specific arrangements to share their expertise with other colleagues and classes. In discussing these matters, groups of primary reading co-ordinators raised the following concerns:

1 There is little or no time for in-service work during a busy day. There seems to be too much to do and not enough time to stand back and look at what others are doing. Other teachers are not necessarily free when the co-ordinators are available.
2 There are often unclear lines of responsibility once the job is filled. There are also ambiguities of role in relation to Headteachers and to other co-ordinators.
3 There have been some difficulties of getting general agreement on reading guidelines for the school and although co-ordinators think it is very important to have a single on-going reading policy it is often very difficult to establish a common policy and more difficult still to implement it.

These problems are more concerned with ways and means, but the more specific duties of a co-ordinator have been more clearly defined.

Duties of co-ordinators

Cockroft (DES, 1982) undertook the task of defining the duties of maths co-ordinators, though his report can be applied with equal relevance to teachers with incentive allowances for language and reading:

In our view it should be part of the duties of the Mathematics Co-ordinator to:

- Prepare a scheme of work for the school in consultation with the Headteacher and staff and, where possible, with schools from which the children come and to which they go;
- Provide guidance and support to other members of staff in implementing the scheme of work, both by means of meetings and by working alongside individual teachers;
- Organise and be responsible for procuring, within funds made available, the necessary teaching resources . . . maintain an up to date inventory and ensure that members of staff are aware of how to use the resources which are available;
- Monitor work . . . throughout the school, including methods of assessment and record keeping;
- Assist with the diagnosis of children's learning difficulties and with their remediation;
- Arrange school based in-service training for members of staff as appropriate;
- Maintain liaison with schools from which they come and to which they go, and also with LEA Advisory staff (DES, 1982).

This constitutes a daunting list of duties that encompasses responsibilities to the children as a class teacher and as a specialist teacher; to colleagues for advice and consultation; to other phases in order to encourage continuity; and to other agencies through liaison. It is clear that in order to carry out these duties in a satisfactory manner, teachers with incentive allowances will need to be released from their classes on a programmed basis.

One of the most immediate challenges faced by language consultants is that of sharing with their colleagues an understanding of the structure of the National Curriculum, of its attainment targets and their weightings, and of the associated programmes of study. This 'sharing' is likely to involve considerable responsibility for INSET as well. It will also include the need for agreed 'formative' and 'summative' assessment measures throughout the school. The language/reading consultant is also likely to have an important part to play in the moderation of standardized assessment tasks (SATs).

These then are challenging duties and responsibilities, and co-ordinators will continue to need full backing and support when carrying them out.

Some recommendations

With this in mind, the groups of reading co-ordinators referred to above made the following recommendations:

1 Headteachers should give full backing to co-ordinators to (a) establish a school policy; (b) involve other members of staff under the leadership of the co-ordinator and (c) encourage other colleagues to accept the co-ordinator's collaboration in order to carry out their responsibilities effectively.

   They should be expected and encouraged by Headteachers to work as members of a team and not left in isolation to think up policies and to implement them. For this reason it might be helpful to have an in-service course for both Headteachers and co-ordinators in order to consider this role.
2 Similarly Inspectors and Advisers should involve co-ordinators and Headteachers in joint discussions.
3 The school organisation should facilitate discussions, for example regular staff meetings with pre-arranged discussion topics should be part of the teacher's job. This should offer consultants a focus for discussion and a way to work towards agreement on various policies and practices.
4 Co-ordinators need to be freed occasionally from their class-room commitments in order to work with other colleagues while the pupils are in school; to meet colleagues who are consultants in other schools; to follow their own in-service training needs; to become more aware of outside facilities (relevant exhibitions, reading centres, work in other areas etc).

These recommendations followed a series of meetings with language consultants and reflect their professional needs as they saw them. Many schools now successfully undertake a number of these suggested procedures, but changing pressures on schools and increasing demands upon headteachers and their staffs make it more important than ever that there should be a clearly established and generally understood and accepted role for every reading co-ordinator.

5 Reading within the national curriculum

Part 1 of the 1988 Education Reform Act provided for the establishment of a National Curriculum, including arrangements for assessment and testing. One of its main aims is 'to establish what children should be expected to know, understand and be able to do at the ages of 7, 11, 14 and 16', i.e. what it calls the 'Key' or 'Reporting' stages.

With this aim in view, the Task Group on Assessment and Testing (TGAT) made some important recommendations (see also p. 75). It stated that (DES, 1987a):

> The assessment process itself should not determine what is taught and learned. It should be the servant not the master of the curriculum. . . . It should be an integral part of the educational process, constantly providing both 'feedback' and 'feedforward'.

TGAT rejected the need for norm-referenced tests and supported the use of criterion – referenced measures based upon specific 'targets', which should be viewed as tasks. These recommendations regard the teacher as central to the assessment process, and 'Teachers' ratings of pupils should be used as a fundamental element of the national assessment system.' This on going classroom-based assessment is seen as being 'formative', in that it can form the basis for pupils' future learning needs and teaching programmes. It is also seen as 'summative', indicating that teachers' assessments can be used incrementally to sum up and 'to provide a comprehensive picture of the overall achievement of a child'.

TGAT also recommended that the assessment process should include a combination of continuous class-based work with forms of national external tests – standardized assessment tasks (SATs). It suggested that there should not be a legal requirement for schools to publish results for 7-year-olds, but that totalled (and not individual) results for the other key stages should be made public.

The pattern of assessment which TGAT established was reflected in the reports of the working groups for the three core subjects which followed. Their task was to advise on:

1 *Attainment targets* – 'The knowledge, skills and understanding which pupils of different abilities and maturities are expected to have at the end of each key stage.'
2 *Programmes of study* – 'The matters, skills and processes which are required to be taught to pupils of different abilities and maturities during each key stage.'

For the English curriculum, the Kingman Committee of Inquiry was set up, one of its main aims being to recommend 'a model' of the English language. This followed the responses to *Curriculum Matters 1: English from 5 to 16* (DES, 1987b), which recommended that a national enquiry should be set up in order to consider what should be taught about language. The Kingman Report emphasized the importance of the interrelationships between reading and the other language modes, and stressed the value of using a wide range of books. Although not tackling head on the issue of Knowledge About Language (KAL), it provided a glossary of 22 language terms for teachers to use.

Immediately following the publication of the Kingman Report, the Cox Working Group was set up. After the publication of its preliminary report (DES, 1988b), the main report was concerned with attainment targets and programmes of study for children aged 5–16 (DES, 1989a).

Attainment targets

Attainment targets are classified under three profile components: speaking and listening, reading, and writing. Aimed at knowledge, skills and attitudes, the different levels of attainment and overall pupil progress will be registered on a 10-point scale, covering the years of compulsory schooling. The Attainment Targets (ATs) are considered essential for every pupil, and it is assumed that (DES, 1989a):

> All or virtually all children will travel along broadly the same curricular path in English, but some will move more quickly, and further than others; and some may hover around the level 1 attainments for the whole of their school careers.

The profile component of reading had two attainment targets, which can be summed up as reading for pleasure and reading for information, with a heavier weighting for the first.

After he had received this report and following the recommendations of the National Curriculum Council (NCC), the Secretary of State issued Draft Orders for Key Stage 1 only. These combined the two ATs into a single target and read as follows:

> The development of the ability to read, understand and respond to all types of writing, as well as the development of information retrieval strategies for the purposes of study (DES, 1989b).

Levels 1–5 are related to the 5- to 11-year-old age group, and range from Level 1(ii) – 'Begin to recognise individual words or letters in familiar contexts' –

to Level 5(ii) – 'Demonstrate, in talking about fiction and poetry, that they are developing their own views and can support them by reference to some details in the text.'

The report is pleased to find references to the importance of English in the reports of other working groups. Reading as a through-curriculum activity is noted in the report on science (DES, 1988c). In its programmes of study, it states that 5- to 7-year-old children 'should develop and use a variety of communication skills and techniques involved in presenting, obtaining and responding to information', and 7- to 11-year-olds 'should be given the opportunity to respond actively and appropriately to information and ideas presented by others'. The need for reading as a means of collecting data is also referred to in the mathematics report (DES, 1988d).

In recording many of the reactions to the second Cox Report (DES, 1989a), the NCC showed an awareness of the importance of reading throughout the curriculum. In its consultation report (NCC, 1989) it showed how statements of attainment could be matched in English, science and mathematics. At level 3, for example, it notes the following uses of study skills:

- *in science* – 'Be able to retrieve and select text, number, sound or graphics stored on a computer.'
- *in English* – 'Select and use effectively appropriate information sources and reference books from the class and school library in order to find out required information.'
- *in mathematics* – 'Extract specific pieces of information from tables and lists. Extract and access information in a simple data base.'

Programmes of study

These describe the ground which must be covered if pupils are to achieve their attainment targets. Cox (DES, 1989a) indicates the need for pupils to experience a broad range of reading materials in order that they can meet these targets. They should include 'carefully selected picture books, nursery rhymes, poems, folk tales, myths and legends and stories with a wide range of settings extending gradually to well chosen children's fiction'. They should also include 'labels, lists, letters, notices, instructions, some newspapers, information books etc'.

The report recommends 'well planned support in developing pleasure and competence', which should involve the teacher reading aloud, reading in groups, sustained silent reading and 'the programme should be planned to encourage children to speculate about what they have read'. The programmes of study summarize many of the sound practices that many classes and schools are already undertaking, but help to add a national dimension to these practices. Among the Draft Orders in Council which followed the NCC Report (1989), the following aims are stated:

The Programmes of Study should teach pupils to:

1 Appreciate the significance of print and the fact that pictures and other visual media can also convey meaning e.g. road signs, logos;
2 Develop an increasing vocabulary of words recognised on sight;
3 Use, as appropriate, all the available clues, such as pictures, context, phonic cues, word shapes and meaning of a passage to decipher new words;
4 Be ready to make informed guesses, and to correct themselves in the light of additional information e.g. by reading ahead or by looking back in the text;
5 Develop the capacity to convey, when reading aloud, the meaning of the text clearly to the listener through intonation and phrasing;
6 Develop the habit of silent reading.

Assessment

As previously mentioned in the section on assessment (see pp. 75–81), this is an area which is likely to be subject to major changes following TGAT and Cox. While teachers see ongoing assessment as a part of their normal teaching responsibilities, there will be a need for increased standardization if the observations of individual teachers are to be validated at school level. There is likely to be a move towards common approaches in the use of IRIs, for example, and reading records will need to be acceptable and usable. Recording will be of particular importance in the moderation of levels of achievement.

Consortia are devising SATs which will be used for 7-year-olds for the first time in 1991. It is important that these should not be seen to take up a great deal of additional school time, and that other curriculum aspects are not eroded as a result of their introduction. Once these SATs have been devised, they will be used as the raw materials for major INSET programmes.

With the beginning of the implementation of the National Curriculum for the core subjects in autumn 1989, there has been very limited time in which to come to terms with what the various reports recommend and what the Secretary of State (with some amendments) has legalized through his statutory Orders.

As was earlier suggested, the immediate challenge is not that of the Attainment Targets nor the Programmes of Study. In reading it is more likely to be the assessment procedures. If these are going to continue to be classroom based, then from the beginning there will need to be agreement on ways and means, and costs will need to be carefully considered.

References

Adams, A. and Jones, E. (1983). *Teaching Humanities in the Microelectronic Age.* Open University Press, Milton Keynes.

Allen, D. (1988). *English Whose English?* National Association of Advisers in English, Doncaster.

Bennett, J. (1979). *Learning to Read with Picture Books.* Thimble Press, Stroud.

Blishen, E. (1974). The unrespectable library. *The School Librarian* 22(3), 216–17.

British Psychological Society (1986). *Achievement in Primary Schools*, Evidence to the House of Commons' Third Report from the Education, Science and Arts Committee, Session 1985–6.

Cambridge Seminar (1987). Evidence given to the Kingman Committee of Inquiry.

Chambers, A. (1973). *Introducing Books to Children.* Heinemann, London.

Cheyney, A. (1971). *Teaching Reading Skills through a Newspaper.* IRA, Newark, Delaware.

Clark, M. (1976). *Young Fluent Readers.* Heinemann, London.

County of Avon (1987). *Guidelines for English and Multi-cultural Education.* Education Department, Bristol.

Coventry Community Education Development Centre (1984). *Reading Involving Parents.* CCEDC, Coventry.

Department of Education and Science (1966). *Children and Their Primary Schools* (The Plowden Report). HMSO, London.

Department of Education and Science (1975). *A Language for Life* (The Bullock Report). HMSO, London.

Department of Education and Science (1978). *Primary Education in England: A Survey by HM Inspectors of Schools.* HMSO, London.

Department of Education and Science (1980). *A View of the Curriculum.* HMSO, London.

Department of Education and Science (1981). *Language Performance in Schools.* Primary Survey Reports 1 and 2. HMSO, London.

Department of Education and Science (1982). *Mathematics Counts* (The Cockroft Report). HMSO, London.

Department of Education and Science (1983a). *9–13 Middle Schools: An Illustrative Survey.* HMSO, London.

Department of Education and Science (1983b). *Teaching Quality.* HMSO, London.

Department of Education and Science (1984). *Education Observed 2.* HMSO, London.

Department of Education and Science (1985a). *Education 8 to 12 in Combined and Middle Schools: An HMI Survey.* HMSO, London.

Department of Education and Science (1985b). *Education Observed 3.* HMSO, London.

Department of Education (1986). *APU Language Testing an Independent Appraisal of Findings.* HMSO, London.

Department of Education and Science (1987a). *Report of the Task Group on Assessment and Testing (TGAT).* HMSO, London.

Department of Education and Science (1987b). *Reading Within the National Curriculum. Curriculum Matters 1: English from 5 to 16.* HMSO, London.

Department of Education and Science (1988a). *Report of the Committee of Inquiry into the Teaching of the English Language* (The Kingman Report). HMSO, London.

Department of Education and Science (1988b). *English for Ages 5 to 11* (The Cox Report Stage 1). HMSO, London.

Department of Education and Science (1988c). *Science for Ages 5 to 16.* HMSO, London.

Department of Education and Science (1988d). *Mathematics for Ages 5 to 16.* HMSO, London.

Department of Education and Science (1989a). *English for Ages 5 to 16.* HMSO, London.

Department of Education and Science (1989b). *English in the National Curriculum* (Statutory Instruments for Key Stage 1). HMSO, London.

Donaldson, M. (1978). *Children's Minds.* Fontana, London.

Friend, P. (1983). Reading and the parent after the Haringey Project. *Reading,* 17(1), 7–12.

Goodman, K. (1964). A linguistic study of cues and miscues. Paper presented to the Educational Research Association, Chicago, February.

House of Commons (1986). *Achievement in Primary Schools* (Third Report of the Education, Science and Arts Committee). HMSO, London.

Inner London Education Authority (1985). *Improving Primary Schools* (The Thomas Report). ILEA, London.

Inner London Education Authority (1986). *The Junior School Project.* Research and Statistics Branch, ILEA, London.

Inner London Education Authority (1988a). *Primary Language Record.* Centre for Language, ILEA, London.

Inner London Education Authority (1988b). *Secondary Transfer Project.* Research and Statistics Branch, ILEA, London.

Jenkinson, A. (1940). *What Do Boys and Girls Read?* Methuen, London.

Jenkinson, M. (1972). Sources of knowledge for theories of reading. In *Reading Today and Tomorrow* (A. Melnick and J. Merritt, eds). ULP, with Oxford University Press, Oxford.

Jones, A. and Buttery, H. (1970). *Children and Stories.* Blackwell, Oxford.

Lavender, R. (1985). Children and books. *Primary Education Review* (NUT), 23 November, 8–10.

London Borough of Newham (1983). *Using Language in Schools.* LBN, London.

London Borough of Newham (1989). *Family Reading Book.* LBN, London.

Lunzer, E. and Gardner, K. (1979). *Effective Use of Reading.* Heinemann for the Schools Council, London.

Mackay, D., Thompson, B. and Schaub, P. (1970). *Breakthrough to Literacy.* Longman for the Schools Council, London.

Meek, M. (1972). The many and the few. *The School Librarian,* 20(1), 8–15.

Meek, M., Warlow, A. and Barton, G. (1977). *The Cool Web.* Bodley Head, London.

94   READING WITHIN AND BEYOND THE CLASSROOM

Melnick, A. and Merritt, J. (1972). *The Reading Curriculum*. Open University Press, Milton Keynes.
Moon, C. (1977). *Individualised Reading*. Ward Lock, London.
Moon, C. (1988). Letter. *Times Educational Supplement* 22 January.
Morgan, R. T. (1976). Paired reading tuition: A preliminary report on a technique for cases of reading deficit. *Child Care, Health and Development* 2, 13–28.
Moss, E. (1979). The audience for children's books. Address to the Library of Congress, National Book League, Washington DC, 12–13 March.
Mudd, N. (1987). Strategies used in the early stages of reading. *Educational Research*, **29**, 83–94.
NATE (1979). *English in Education*. Aberdeen University Press, Aberdeen.
NATE (1986). *English Teaching and the New Technology into the 1990's*. NATE, Sheffield.
National Curriculum Council (1989). *A Framework for the Primary Curriculum*. NCC, London.
Newham In-Service Education Centre (1988). *Newham Reading Programme*. LBN, London.
Newham Parents' Centre (1983). *Books, Schools and the Urban Community*. LBN, London.
Northern Ireland Council for Educational Development (1985). *Guidelines for Primary Schools: Language and Literacy*. Learning Resources Unit, Stranmillis College, Belfast.
Opie, I. and Opie, P. (1976). *The Classic Fairy Tales*. Oxford University Press, Oxford.
Perera, K. (1987). *Understanding Language*. National Association of Advisers in English, Doncaster.
Primary English Teaching Association (1985). *Computers and Language*. PETA, Rozelle, New South Wales.
Pumphrey, P. (1986). Paired reading and pitfalls. *Educational Research*, **28**(2), 89–94.
Robinson, F. (1961). *Effective Study*. Harper and Row, New York.
Robinson, H. (1964). Developing critical reading. In *Dimensions of Critical Reading* (R. Stauffer, ed.). IRA, Newark, Delaware.
Robinson, H. (1972). Developing critical reading. In *The Reading Curriculum* (A. Melnick and J. Merritt, eds). ULP/Open University Press, Milton Keynes.
Robson, D., Miller, A. and Bushell, R. (1984). The development of paired reading in High Peak and West Derbyshire. *Remedial Education* **19**.
Sampson, G. (1952). *English for the English*. Cambridge University Press, Cambridge.
Smith, F. (1971). *Understanding Reading*. Holt, Rinehart and Winston, New York.
Southgate, V., Arnold, H. and Johnson, S. (1981). *Extending Beginning Reading*. Heinemann for the Schools Council, London.
Spode, P. (1983). Comics. *Reading*, **7** (2), 67–86.
Stauffer, R. and Cramer, R. (1968). *Teaching Critical Reading at the Primary Level*. IRA, Newark, Delaware.
Strang, R. (1978). The nature of reading. In *Reading from Process to Practice*. Routledge and Kegan Paul, London.
Tiburtis, S. (1988). Letter. *Times Educational Supplement* 22 January.
Thornton, G. (1986). *APU Language Testing 1979–1983: An Independent Appraisal of the Findings*. HMSO, London.
Topping, K. and McKnight, G. (1984). Paired reading- and parent power. *Special Education: Forward Trends*, **11**(3), 12–15.
Newton, M. and Thompson, M. (1976). *The Aston Index*. University of Aston, Birmingham.

Vincent, D. (1985). *Reading Tests in the Classroom: An Introduction.* NFER Nelson, Windsor.

Wade, B. (1989). *Reading for Real.* Open University Press, Milton Keynes.

Walker, C. (1974). *Reading Development and Extension.* Ward Lock, London.

Welton, J. (1906). *Principles and Methods of Teaching.* University Tutorial Press, London.

Whitehead, F. (1975). *Children's Reading Interests.* Methuen for the Schools Council, London.

Whitehead, F. (1977). *Children and Their Books.* Schools Council Research Studies Series. Macmillan, London.

Widlake, P. and Macleod, F. (1984). *Raising Standards.* Coventry Community Education Development Centre, Coventry.

Wray, D. (1982). Research insights into extending reading. *Reading* 16(1), 31–42.

Index

51   5